Heinemann History Scheme

LIFE IN MEDIEVAL TIMES

FOUNDATION

BOOK 1

Fiona Reynoldson

Heinemann Educational Publishers
Halley Court, Jordan Hill, Oxford, OX2 8EJ
a division of Reed Educational & Professional Publishing Ltd
Heinemann is a registered trademark of Reed Educational & Professional Publishing Ltd

OXFORD MELBOURNE AUCKLAND
JOHANNESBURG BLANTYRE GABORONE
IBADAN PORTSMOUTH NH (USA) CHICAGO

© Fiona Reynoldson 2002

First published 2002

ISBN 0 435 32605 8

05 04 03 02
10 9 8 7 6 5 4 3 2 1

Designed and typeset by Visual Image, Taunton

Illustrated by Paul Bale, Jane Durston, Keith Richmond and Ian Heard

Printed and bound in Italy by Printer Trento Srl

Picture research by Diana Phillips

Photographic acknowledgements
The authors and publishers would like to thank the following for permission to reproduce photographs and copyright material:
Aerofilms: p. 65 (both); Art Archive: pp. 21, 36, 53, 58, 100 (left), 108 (top); Bridgeman Art Library: pp. 16, 66, 80, 106, 139, 142, 148, 149, 189, 190; British Library: pp. 105 (both), 107 (both); Bodleian Library: pp. 108 (bottom), 117; Buckinghamshire Record Office: p. 67; Collections: p. 91 (bottom); Corpus Christi College, Cambridge: p. 183; Fotomas: p. 154; Sonia Halliday: pp. 72, 87, 90 (all), 91 (top), 94 (both), 98, 168, 169, 172, 173, 177 (top), 191; M Holford: pp. 29, 30; A F Kersting: pp. 34, 44, 100 (bottom); Kobal: p. 84; Photodisc: p. 15; Punch: p. 17; Rex Features/Sipa: p. 184; Saltaire Village Society: p. 24 (top); Science Photo Library: p. 18; Skyscan: pp. 22, 74; Spectrum: pp. 24 (bottom), 174 (both).

Cover photograph: © The Bodleian Library

Maps and realia
Map reproduced from Ordnance Survey maps with the permission of The Controller of Her Majesty's Stationery Office © Crown Copyright: p. 35; English Heritage: p. 103 (bottom); Whee Ky Ma: p. 14 (top).

Written source acknowledgements
The authors and publishers gratefully acknowledge the following publications from which written sources in the book are drawn. In some sources the wording or sentence has been simplified.
H S Bennett, *Life on the English Manor*, Cambridge University Press, 1937: p. 95 (bottom left)
M T Clanchy, *England and its rulers*, Fontana 1983: p. 33
R J Cootes, *The Middle Ages*, Longman, 1972: p. 66 (top right)
A H Dodd, *Life in Elizabethan England*, Batsford, 1961: p. 133
G Evans, *Pilgrimages and Crusades*, 1976: p. 184 (left)
H E Hallam, *Rural England*, Fontana, 1981: p. 66 (top left)
A Harmsworth, *Elizabethan England*, John Murray, 1999: p. 141
T Jones & A Ereria, *The Crusades*, BBC Books, 1994: pp. 164, 184 (right)
M H Keen, *England in the Later Middle Ages*, Routledge, 1973: p. 95 (bottom right)
J Kerr, *The Crusades*, Wheaton, 1966: p. 179
B Lewis, *Islam, from the Prophet Muhammad to the capture of Constantinople*, Harper & Row, 1974: p. 162
H R Loyn, *Anglo-Saxon England and the Norman Conquest*, Longman, 1962: p. 66 (bottom right)
J Nicol, *The Tudors*, Blackwell, 1981: p. 155 (bottom)
G Regan, *Elizabethan England*, Batsford, 1990: p. 138 (top)
P Servini, *The English Reformation*, Hodder & Stoughton, 1997: p. 131 (both)
C Shepherd (ed.), *Contrasts and connections*, John Murray, 1991: pp. 50, 51
C Shepherd et al, *Societies in change*, John Murray, 1992: p. 137 (bottom)
S Styles, *Elizabethan England*, Heinemann, 1992: pp. 137 (top), 138 (bottom), 155 (top)
The Times, 5 June 1913: p. 15 (right)
The Times, 1987: p. 105 (bottom)
The Mirror, 14 February 2000: p. 19
D Wilkinson & J Cantrell, *Normans in Britain*, Macmillan Press Ltd, 1987: pp. 41, 62, 64.

Contents

Unit 1: Introductory unit – what's it all about?

SWEDEN

FINLAND

RUSSIA

ESTONIA
LATVIA
BELARUS
ND
UKRAINE
HUNGARY
ROMANIA
BULGARIA
REECE
TURKEY

KAZAKSTAN

MONGOLIA

NORTH
KOREA
JAPAN

SOUTH
KOREA

PACIFIC
OCEAN

TURKMENISTAN
UZBEKISTAN
KYRGYZSTAN

SYRIA
IRAQ
IRAN
AFGHANISTAN
PAKISTAN

CHINA

NEPAL
BHUTAN

LAOS

YA
EGYPT
SAUDI
ARABIA

INDIA
MYANMAR

VIETNAM

PHILIPPINES

OMAN

ERITREA
SOUTHERN YEMEN
YEMEN

BANGLADESH
THAILAND
CAMBODIA

HAD
SUDAN
SOMALIA

CENTRAL
AFRICAN
REPUBLIC
ETHIOPIA

MALAYSIA

UGANDA
KENYA
DEM. REP.
OF THE
CONGO
RWANDA
BURUNDI
TANZANIA
MALAWI

INDONESIA

PAPUA
NEW
GUINEA

INDIAN
OCEAN

OLA
ZAMBIA

MOZAMBIQUE

MADAGASCAR

NEW
CALEDONIA

AUSTRALIA

SWAZILAND
SOUTH
AFRICA
LESOTHO

NEW
ZEALAND

SOUTHERN OCEAN

TIMELINES

5000BC – 2000AD

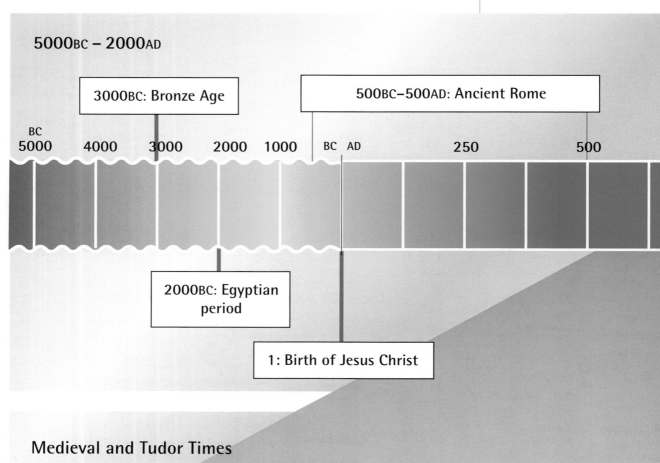

3000BC: Bronze Age

500BC–500AD: Ancient Rome

BC
5000   4000   3000   2000   1000   BC   AD   250   500

2000BC: Egyptian period

1: Birth of Jesus Christ

Medieval and Tudor Times

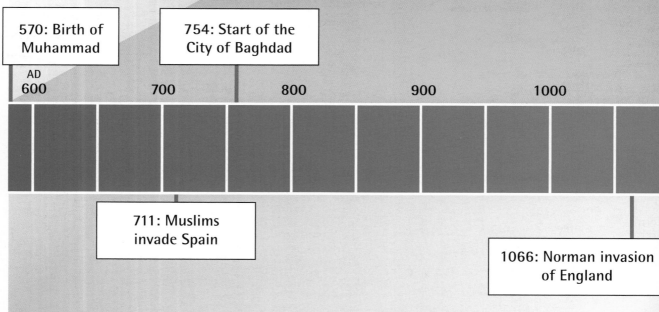

570: Birth of Muhammad

754: Start of the City of Baghdad

AD
600   700   800   900   1000

711: Muslims invade Spain

1066: Norman invasion of England

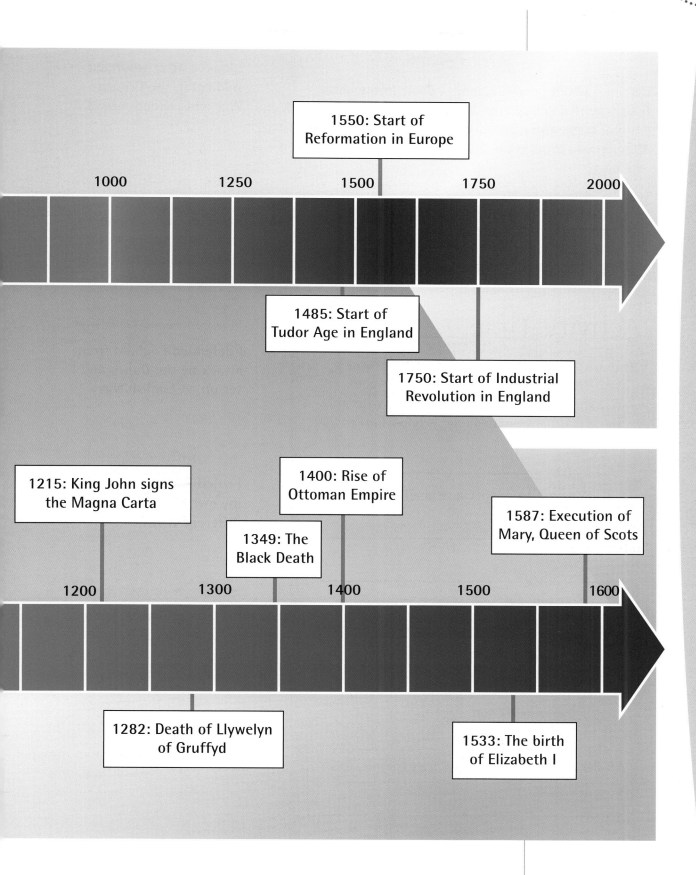

WHO IS THE MOST IMPORTANT PERSON I KNOW ABOUT IN HISTORY?

History is about people. Famous people in the past have invented and discovered great things. They have fought, made peace and ruled countries and empires. Who do you think is the most important person in the past?

What does it mean?

Empire
A group of countries ruled by one person.

Activity Time

1 Think of someone who is important to you. Write out the sentence below in your book. Fill in the name of the person and then write in three reasons why he or she is important to you.

_____

is important to me because she/he

1 _____

2 _____

3 _____

2 Draw the chart below in your book. Then look at Source 1 and match the people from history to their achievements.

Person	What are they famous for?

SOURCE 1

I looked after wounded soldiers in the Crimean War and trained nurses.

I was an explorer and sailed around the world. I fought against the Spanish Armada.

I defended England from attack by the Danes and I set up an English Navy.

I ruled England and set up my own Church. I had six different wives.

I ruled the Roman Empire. I was murdered by some rivals.

I invented a steam locomotive.

FLORENCE NIGHTINGALE

QUEEN VICTORIA

ALEXANDER THE GREAT

I wrote many plays that are still popular today.

HENRY VIII

SIR FRANCIS DRAKE

WILLIAM SHAKESPEARE

I was King of Greece and conquered Persia and Egypt.

I tried to blow up the Houses of Parliament but I was caught and executed.

GEORGE STEPHENSON

GUY FAWKES

KING ALFRED

I ruled for 64 years when Britain had an empire all over the world.

I led a revolt against the Romans. I poisoned myself rather than be captured.

JULIUS CAESAR

BOUDICCA

ELIZABETH 1

I made England wealthy and successful when I was queen.

TIME CHECK

To help us to make sense of the past, we split it up into different time periods or eras. Periods can be named after what objects were made from at that time, like the Stone Age. They can also be named after which family was in charge, like the Tudor Age.

CENTURIES AND DECADES

Sometimes to be more exact about time, we use centuries. A century is one hundred years. The sixteenth century is the hundred years from 1500 to 1599. For smaller time periods we use decades. The 1990s is the decade or ten years from 1990 to 1999.

Activity Time

1 Dates are sometimes written next to the letters BC or AD. BC means 'Before Christ'. AD means 'Anno Domini' which is Latin for 'in the year of Our Lord'. Find out why dates are written with these letters.

2 Some periods have been labelled on the timeline on pages 6 and 7, but there are many more. Write out each of the periods below on a piece of paper and place them in chronological order on the timeline. Chronological order means the order that the periods came in.

a   Iron Age – 500 BC to 43 AD

b   Viking Age – 750 to 1000 AD

c   Eighteenth century

d   The Middle Ages – 1066 to 1485

e   The 1960s

f   Victorian Age – 1837 to 1901

Activity Time

Famous people, famous times

1 Look at pages 8 and 9 and write each person's name on a slip of paper. Then, for each person, find out when they lived and write the century in which they lived below each name. For example:

> Florence Nightingale
>
> nineteenth century

2 Now place each slip of paper in the correct place on the timeline on pages 6 and 7. Which time period were most of these people living in?

3 Work in pairs to decide who is the most important person in history. It does not have to be anyone from pages 8 and 9 and you can disagree with your partner. Discuss all the different reasons why you have chosen your person to appear in History's Hall of Fame.

4 a Draw a sketch of your chosen person to hang in History's Hall of Fame. Include a decorated picture frame to make them look important. The frame could be decorated with pictures or objects from their life and work.

IMPORTANT PEOPLE

Which people are important in history? Inventors, explorers, kings, queens, leaders of armies and writers have all had important roles in history.

Activity Time

Who do the people in your class think are the top three most important people in history? Do a survey to find out. How many chose people who:

   a are important for making their country great?

   b are important for helping people?

c are important because they changed history?

d are important because they were very talented?

e are important because they were brave?

Did anyone in your class have any other reasons?

b Write a sentence to say what the person is famous for.

c Write a sentence saying why you think the person is so important. Give two reasons.

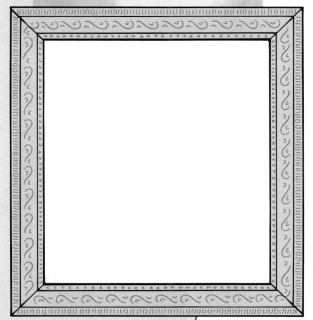

Who deserves to appear in History's Hall of Fame?

MAKING A DIFFERENCE

Read about these four people and decide what difference they made to history.

SOURCE 2

JULIUS CAESAR

Julius Caesar was a Roman leader. He was famous for winning battles and gaining land for Rome to rule. He ruled the Roman Empire from 46 to 44 BC. He was stabbed to death by enemies.

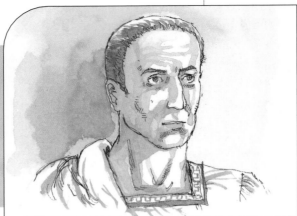

SOURCE 3

QUEEN ELIZABETH I

Elizabeth ruled England from 1558 to 1603. She made England a Protestant country and brought in laws to look after the poor. She encouraged exploration and trade so that England became a wealthy nation. She encouraged plays and poems to be written. In 1588, during her rule the navy stopped the Spanish Armada from invading England. She executed a lot of people, including her cousin, Mary, Queen of Scots.

SOURCE 4

GUY FAWKES

Guy Fawkes was a Catholic and was unhappy about King James' bad treatment of Catholics. He was involved in a plot to blow up Parliament and the king in November 1605 but was caught in a cellar underneath the Houses of Parliament with some explosives. He was tortured and executed. The plot made Catholics more unpopular in England. He is still remembered on 5 November each year on Bonfire Night.

SOURCE 5

GEORGE STEPHENSON
George Stephenson was an engineer. He invented the first successful steam locomotive, called 'The Rocket'. He designed the style of railway tracks now used all over the world. He worked for one of the first railway companies in England, on the Manchester to Liverpool line. He helped to make travel much quicker.

Activity Time

1 Copy and fill in the chart to show what difference each person made to the world.

Person	This person made a big difference to the world by...
Julius Caesar	
Queen Elizabeth I	
Guy Fawkes	
George Stephenson	

Summary

When you come across new people in history remember to think about:
• why they are important
• what effect they had on history.

2 Which of the four people do you think made the most difference to how we live today?

3 How many people on the chart on pages 8 and 9 are women? Why do you think that there are more famous men in history than women?

WHAT ARE WE GOING TO FIND OUT ABOUT IN HISTORY IN YEARS 7, 8 AND 9?

We find out about what happened in history from many different types of evidence. These are called sources. Sources can be:

- written (for example, letters)
- visual (for example, photographs)
- oral (for example, people speaking)
- artefacts (for example, pottery)

See if you can think of at least six other sources that historians might use to find out about the past. Try to think of some written, some visual and some oral sources.

Now look at Sources 1 to 8.

SOURCE 1

The home page of one of the Anne Frank websites.

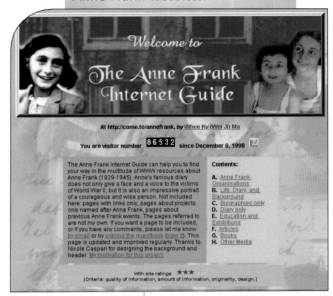

SOURCE 2

A painting of the storming of the Bastille during the French Revolution, which started in 1789.

What does it mean?

Source
A piece of evidence which can tell us about history.

SOURCE 3

I have a dream that my four little children will one day live in a nation where they will not be judged by the colour of their skin but by the content of their character.

Part of Martin Luther King's 'I have a dream' speech made in the 1960s.

SOURCE 4

The desperate act of a woman who rushed from the rails on to the course so that she could spoil the race. She was trampled by the king's horse. She is in the Suffragist* movement. We think that yesterday's exhibition does more harm than good to the cause of votes for women.

*Suffragist – person who wanted women to be allowed to vote.

Taken from *The Times* newspaper of 5 June 1913, about the death of Emily Davison at the Derby horse race.

SOURCE 5

A twentieth-century photograph of the Taj Mahal in India, which was built in the seventeenth century.

A painting of the
execution of Mary,
Queen of Scots in 1587.

Den VIII february werde onthalst Maria
Stuart Schots Coninginne s'teruende Roomsch Catho-

Activity Time

1 Look at Sources 1 to 7. Match the headlines to the correct
source numbers.

**Shock! Horror! France is
turned upside down**

Girl caught up in war

**Off with her head — Queen has
cousin executed**

Thousands dying of disease

**Beautiful tomb built for dead
queen as love gift**

**Dying Emily says:
Give women the vote!**

One man's dream

SOURCE 7

A nineteenth-century cartoon called 'A Court for King Cholera'.
It shows a London Street.

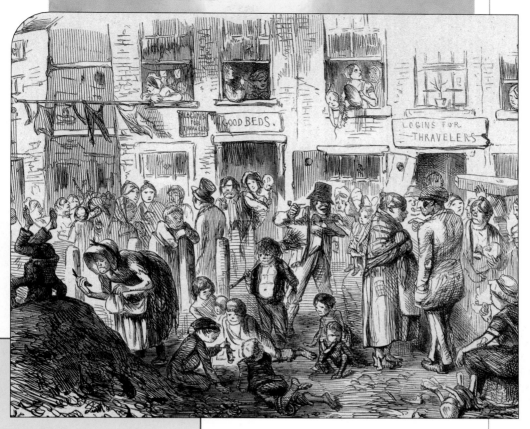

2 Choose one of the sources. What does it show or describe?

3 Look at the timeline on pages 6 and 7. On a slip of paper write the source number and put it in the correct place on the timeline. From what time do most of the sources come?

4 On the same slips of paper, now write down the country that each source came from. Place your slips of paper on the correct places on the map on pages 4 and 5.

FANCY A CHALLENGE?

Copy this chart and fill it in for Sources 2–7. Source 1 is filled in as an example of what you need to do.

Number	Type	What is it about?	What clues does it give?
1	Website	Anne Frank	It tells us who Anne Frank was and how to find out more information about her. It shows us that the person making the website sees her as a victim of the Second World War.

PROBLEMS WITH EVIDENCE

Some sources may not tell us the whole truth and so may not be reliable (trustworthy). Source 8 below is not reliable. It was faked in 1912. Source 7 may or may not be reliable. To check that sources are reliable we have to ask questions. If a source is not reliable then it may not be useful or relevant for helping us understand the past. Here are three of the questions we might ask:

- Who made the source?
- When was it made?
- Why was it made?

By asking these questions we are building up an interpretation of a source. This means we can explain the meaning of the source.

SOURCE 8

A reconstruction of Piltdown Man's skull found in 1912. People claimed the skull was the link between humans and apes. In 1953 scientists discovered that the skull was a fake. The skull fragments were human but the jaw belonged to an ape.

Question Time

1 Look at Source 7.

  a What makes you think death is usual in this area? Is the recent death an adult or a child?

  b What makes you think the street is very dirty?

  c What makes you think that people are very poor? Find as many things as you can.

  d What does the artist who drew the picture want you to think?

2 Why is it important to know who made a source before we can use it as a piece of reliable and useful evidence?

WHAT'S HISTORY GOT TO DO WITH ME?

HISTORY EXPLAINS THE PRESENT

You will have seen or heard news about the peace process in Northern Ireland on the television or radio. The problems between Catholics and Protestants in Northern Ireland have been in the news for many years now. Source 1 below is written for readers of newspapers. It does not tell you about the background to the problems. You would need to know this background or history to understand what is going on today.

SOURCE 1

IRA Guns Deal Hope

General John de Chastelain is said to have received private documents from an IRA go-between. The papers are believed to include details of a timetable for the hand-over of terrorist guns and explosives. The general said that this was strong enough to bring back the power-sharing ruling council in Northern Ireland. The Ulster Unionists called the secret IRA offer a 'gimmick'.

Adapted from an extract from *The Mirror* newspaper, 14/2/00.

Question Time

Read Source 1.

1. Who gave the general the private documents?

2. What do the papers include?

3. Find evidence that the journalist is not sure about the story (there are at least two phrases in the source).

4. Think of five things you would like to ask so that you could understand the article.

Question Time

Look again at Source 1 on page 19. Are you still confused about the story? How could you find out more?

❶ Write down five things you would like to ask about the newspaper article so that you can understand the story.

❷ You are a television news reporter. Your task is to film a programme which will tell people the full story behind the article.

   a Which people would you like to interview in your programme?

   b List three questions for each person you have decided to interview.

   c What would you like to include in the introduction to your programme?

   d How would you find the information for this introduction?

❸ Look at a newspaper and select an article which does not tell you all you need to know.

   a Write down five questions you would like to ask.

   b Which sources would you use to help you find out more?

You will now see that it is very important to understand the past, if we want to understand what is going on today. Almost all events which take place today are affected by something which has happened in the past.

Summary

- We need history to understand what's happening today.
- To find out about events we have to ask questions.
- We can get answers from many types of sources.
- We may need several sources to build up a picture of the past.

VISITING THE PAST

Some historic buildings are modernised and people live in them. Some are preserved as they would have been in the past and are opened to the public so we can understand our history. The National Trust and English Heritage look after many historic places. We can use historic sites, like factories, churches, castles, markets and streets to find out about the past. Just like written sources or pictures, we have to look at the evidence carefully and search for clues. By asking questions we can learn from the buildings we visit.

VISIT NUMBER 1 – THE MIDDLE AGES

On this page and the next there are two photographs and a plan of Fountains Abbey. In Source 4 there is an information box about Fountains Abbey. See how much you can find out by looking, reading and asking questions.

What does it mean?

Site
The place that something is found or built.

SOURCE 1

A photograph of Fountains Abbey.

THE ABBEY AS EVIDENCE

On page 23 you will find an Evidence Sheet. By answering the questions you will be gathering evidence from Sources 1 to 3. As you look at the photographs and the plan think about:

- the size of the rooms
- the materials
- what is missing.

On page 23 you will find an Evidence Sheet.

SOURCE 2

An aerial photograph of Fountains Abbey.

SOURCE 3

A plan of Fountains Abbey.

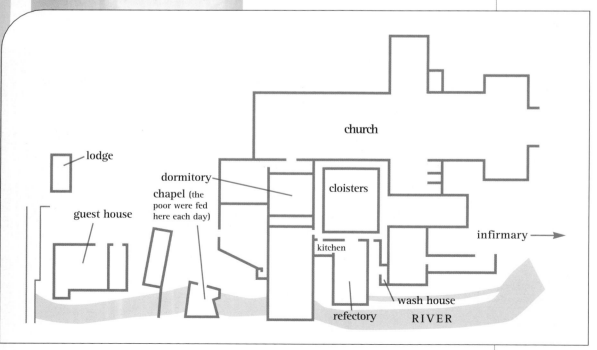

FILLING IN THE EVIDENCE SHEET

Copy the Evidence Sheet, then fill it in.

SOURCE 4

Information Box

Fountains Abbey is in North Yorkshire. It was founded (set up) in 1132 by a group of monks. They wanted to live quietly, working and praying to God. At first they probably lived in wooden huts and built a wooden church. After a few years they built a huge abbey made of stone. Fountains Abbey would have held up to 250 monks at one time. Monks lived and worked there until 1536, when Henry VIII closed down the monastery and took its wealth.

Evidence Sheet:

Looking

1 a What is the abbey made of?

   b Which is the largest building in the abbey?

   c Where is the abbey built? Is it:

   • on a hill
   • in a valley
   • by the sea
   • near other buildings
   • near a river
   • near woodland?

   d Write down at least two other things you have noticed in Sources 1 to 3.

Thinking

2 a Why do you think the monks chose this site for their abbey?

   b Write down three questions you would like to ask. (For example, why is the abbey in ruins?)

   c Read Source 4. Does this answer any of your questions?

Other Sources

3 What other sources would we want to look for to help us find out more?

Conclusions

4 What does the site tell us? Does it tell us:

   • how monks lived
   • what was important to monks
   • that monasteries were rich?

VISIT NUMBER 2 – THE NINETEENTH CENTURY

The second example is part of the unusual village of Saltaire in Yorkshire.

MAKING YOUR OWN EVIDENCE SHEET

Copy the example of the Evidence Sheet on page 23. Put in the headings: Looking, Thinking, Other Sources and Conclusions. Then fill it in using the questions in the Question Time box on page 25 to help you.

Copy the example of the Evidence Sheet on page 23.

SOURCE 5

A photograph of houses at Saltaire.

Information Box

Saltaire was a village built by Sir Titus Salt. He wanted to build a clean, well laid out village for the workers in his textile (cloth) mills. It was built between 1851 and 1872.

SOURCE 6

Part of the textile mill in Saltaire. The windows are large compared to other buildings at the time.

SOURCE 7

A plan of Saltaire showing the mill, the workers' houses and the leisure facilities.

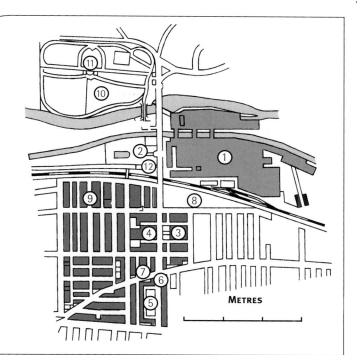

① The Mill
② Church
③ The Institute (for adult learning)
④ The School
⑤ The Almshouses (for poor people)
⑥ The Hospital
⑦ Chapel
⑧ Sunday School
⑨ The Bath and Washhouse
⑩ The Park
⑪ Statue of Sir Titus Salt
⑫ Workers' Dining Room
▮ Workers' Houses

You can do this sort of task for any historic site or building. Think of historic buildings in your area, like a church. Put the information you can find out about it in a chart like the one below.

Place from the past	Time period/s	What can it tell us about?

Summary

In this section you have learned that:
- buildings can be used as evidence of the past
- we have to look at them carefully
- we can ask questions about buildings
- history is all around us.

Question Time

Looking

What is the street like? What are the buildings made of? Make a list of the buildings in Saltaire that are to do with work, religion, education, sickness and poverty and everyday living.

Thinking

What evidence is there that the houses were heated by coal fires? Why do you think the windows in Source 6 are large? What other things would you like to know?

Other sources

What other sources would you like to see?

Conclusions

What was it like to live and work there?

Unit 2: How did medieval monarchs keep control?

In this Unit you are going to learn about how monarchs (kings and queens) ruled their people and lands. At the end of the Unit you are going to answer an important question: how did medieval monarchs keep control?

I OBEY BECAUSE IF I DON'T THEY'LL CHOP MY HEAD OFF...

EXCITING TIMES!

During medieval times (the Middle Ages) at least three monarchs were murdered, one of them with a red-hot poker. One king was so nervous that he slept with weapons under his bed. Another king fought a war against his wife and sons. At least three kings totally lost control of their kingdoms during the Middle Ages.

Some monarchs were better at keeping control than others. Some monarchs were able to solve many of the problems to do with land, rich people, poor people, religion and crime. Different monarchs used different ways to get their people to obey them.

I OBEY BECAUSE MY RELIGION TELLS ME TO...

OBEYING THE RULER

Throughout history people have obeyed their rulers for different reasons. In the Middle Ages, people obeyed for a mixture of reasons.

I OBEY BECAUSE I GET SOMETHING OUT OF IT...

I OBEY BECAUSE I KNOW MY PLACE

Activity Time

In this unit, you need to understand these words:

power, control, conqueror, monarch, ruler, invasion, defence, attack, conquest.

❶ Look each word up in a dictionary. Draw pictures to illustrate the meaning of three of the words.

❷ See if the other people in the class can work out which words you have drawn pictures for.

HOW DID WILLIAM OF NORMANDY TAKE CONTROL OF ENGLAND?

WINNING THE WAR

In the late summer of 1066, William of Normandy (a place in northern France) landed in the south of England with a large army.

In October 1066, William won the Battle of Hastings and marched to London.

On Christmas Day 1066, William was crowned King of England in Westminster Abbey in London. William's take-over of England is known as the Norman Conquest. A conquest is when a person or army defeats the enemy. William is known as William the Conqueror.

WINNING THE PEACE

William had won the war. Now he had to win the peace. It would have been difficult to rule by forcing people to obey – too many soldiers would be needed! Instead, William had to persuade people to obey him. Your task is to look out for all the different abilities that William had which made him successful in war and peace. Look out for the following qualities:

- clever ideas
- determination
- being prepared
- support from others.

In this Unit you will also find out how William became king.

Question Time

❶ Which battle did William win?

❷ Where and when was William crowned King of England?

❸ Apart from the qualities shown at the bottom of the page, what other qualities might a ruler or leader need? Think of leaders that are familiar to you (headteacher, prime minister). What qualities do they have?

WHAT HAPPENED AS EDWARD LAY DYING?

The year before William the Conqueror was crowned King of England, King Edward lay dying. Who would be the next king? Edward had no children to take the throne. The great men of England were worried. They did not want a foreign king. He would bring foreign soldiers and foreign nobles into England. There were three main contenders for the throne.

1066 – WHO WOULD BECOME KING OF ENGLAND?

Duke William of Normandy

I am cousin to King Edward. He promised me the throne. I am a skilled soldier and I have my own army.

Harald Hardrada, King of Norway

I am descended from King Canute who ruled England before King Edward. This means I have the right to be King of England.

Harold Godwinson, Earl of Wessex

My sister is King Edward's wife. The king promised me the throne just before he died. I am rich and powerful and I have my own army.

KING HAROLD

On the day of King Edward's funeral, the Witan (the great men of England who made up the king's council of advisers) crowned Harold Godwinson as King of England.

What does it mean?

Nobles

Members of the nobility – nobles – are people born into rich and powerful families. These families often have links with royal families.

Question Time

1. What was the Witan?

2. Why do you think the Witan did not want a foreign king?

3. Write down three things that Harold Godwinson might say to show that his claim to be king is better than William's or Hardrada's.

WILLIAM'S INVASION

When William heard that Harold had been crowned King of England, he got ready to invade. Some of Williams' advisers told him it would be too difficult to conquer England. But William was determined!

William's army

William had his own well-trained army of knights, archers and footsoldiers. He made this army bigger by persuading his neighbours to join him. William promised that if they helped him to conquer England, he would give them English land as a reward. By summer William was ready, but for weeks the wind blew in the wrong direction and he could not sail for England.

Hardrada sailed from Norway with Tostig, King Harold's own rebellious brother. King Harold defeated and killed them at Stamford Bridge. Then he heard that William had left St Valery in Normandy, sailed across the English Channel and landed at Pevensey. He quickly marched south to fight William near Hastings.

The events of September and October 1066.

A scene from the Bayeux Tapestry showing trees being cut down for William's boats.

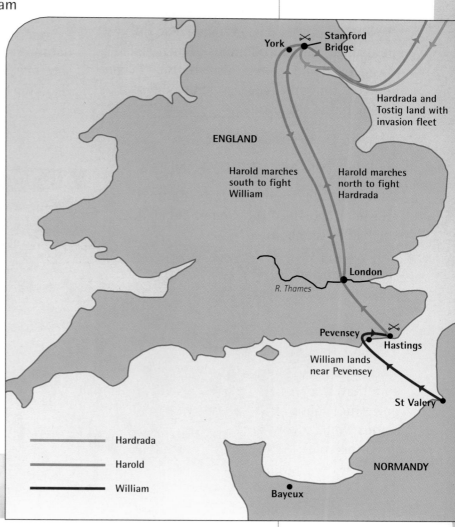

THE BATTLE OF HASTINGS, 14 OCTOBER 1066

Harold's army was grouped on top of Senlac Hill near Hastings. William moved his army into battle order on the ground below Senlac Hill.

The fighting

Harold's best soldiers fought with battleaxes and shields. They had formed a wall so that William's soldiers could not get through. The Norman knights of William's army had to gallop uphill to try to break up the wall. They were driven back and some ran away down the hill. This tempted some of Harold's men to chase them. Seeing this William had a good idea. He ordered some of his soldiers to pretend to run away and again Harold's men chased them. At the bottom of the hill, William's soldiers turned and killed Harold's men.

The end of the battle

By evening, Harold had very few men left. William and his army overran Senlac Hill and killed Harold. Thousands of men had been killed and injured in the battle. William ordered that an abbey should be built as a memorial to those killed.

What does it mean?

Baron
Someone who has power and land, and who usually supported the monarch.

WILLIAM MARCHES TO LONDON

Now that William had won the Battle of Hastings and killed the King of England, he had to set about conquering the rest of England. First, he had to be crowned as King of England. He also needed to make sure that powerful English barons would accept his rule.

SOURCE 2

A scene from the Bayeux Tapestry showing broken bodies on the ground.

William headed for London, passing through important towns like Dover and Canterbury on the way. As he got near to London, William heard that English soldiers were holding London Bridge, so William decided to circle around London. He marched upstream and crossed the River Thames at a place called Wallingford. He arrived at Berkhamsted. On the way he burned some villages and crops.

At Berkhamsted

At Berkhamsted some of the leaders of Harold's army and some of the leaders of the Church came to meet William. They agreed to accept William as king.

The coronation in Westminster Abbey

On 25 December 1066, William was crowned King of England in Westminster Abbey. He told everyone that he was the rightful successor to the throne and that King Edward had promised him the throne. He had also won it by right of conquest. He had gained power and control in England.

Question Time

1. What is the name of the tapestry shown in Sources 1 and 2? Why do you think it is called this?

2. Westminster Abbey was built by King Edward. Why do you think it was important to William that he was crowned there?

3. Find your nearest war memorial.

   a Which war or wars is it dedicated to?

   b What can you learn from it about the past?

   c Why do you think William wanted to put a memorial at Hastings?

Activity Time

Make your own map of what happened in 1066. You need a large blank map like the one on this page.

1. Mark on your map all the towns that are described here.

2. Then look at the map on page 29. Mark the town in Normandy where William sailed from.

3. Now draw in:

   a William's route to Hastings.

   b Harold's routes.

   c Hardrada's route.

   d William's route to London after he had won the Battle of Hastings.

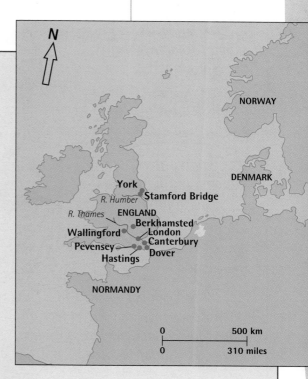

Activity Time

What made William a successful conqueror?

a Copy out the table below. Leave room for 3 blank rows.

b Read the statements below. For each one decide what qualities they show
and put them into the correct column. One is done for you.

Determined	Prepared	Clever	Supported	Lucky
		William was crowned in Westminster Abbey to show he was the rightful king.		

Ignored the advice in Normandy not to invade England.

Harold had to march north and defeat Hardrada just as William was invading in the south.

Got promises of support from neighbours in France.

Took trained soldiers to England.

Prepared food, weapons and horses in Normandy.

Circled around London to enter from the north.

The defeated leaders of Harold's army and the rulers of the Church agreed that William should be king.

Captured the important towns of Dover and Canterbury before he went to London.

HOW DO WE KNOW ABOUT THE NORMAN CONQUEST?

THE BAYEUX TAPESTRY

The Bayeux Tapestry is a long strip of linen material with pictures embroidered on it in different coloured wools. The pictures tell the story of the Norman Conquest. There are 72 pictures. The tapestry is 70 m long and 48 cm tall. The pictures on pages 29 and 30 are from the Bayeux Tapestry. Most of our information about the Battle of Hastings comes from the Bayeaux Tapestry.

Question Time

1 Work in pairs. Look at one of the pictures from the Bayeux Tapestry. Describe what is happening.

2 Make a cartoon strip of the Norman Conquest using just four pictures.

- William builds his ships.
- William lands in England.
- William fights at Hastings.
- William is crowned in Westminster Abbey.

3 Whose version of the Norman Conquest is told in the Bayeux Tapestry? Why do you think this is?

CONTROLLING THE LAND BY BUILDING CASTLES

William built his own royal castles. He also gave English land to his Norman barons. He gave his barons permission to build castles to live in. They wanted to:

- be safe from attack by the English
- show off their power
- control the land and people around the castle.

An artist's reconstruction of a motte and bailey castle.

Question Time

1 Look back at page 33. Why did the Norman barons want to build castles?

2 Look at Source 1. Does this give good evidence to back up your answer to question 1? Explain why.

MOTTE AND BAILEY CASTLES

The first castles were wooden towers that were built on top of earth mounds. They could be built very quickly. Sometimes they had a moat and a high wall around them.

What does it mean?

Motte A high mound which made the castle difficult to attack.

Bailey A fenced area at the bottom of the mound.

Moat A ditch filled with water to protect against attackers.

SOURCE 2

A photo of Berkhamsted motte and bailey castle. Look also at the motte and bailey drawing on page 33.

Why was the motte a steep hill?

Why was there a tower on top of the motte?

What was the tower for?

Why was there a drawbridge?

Why did the motte have a staircase?

What was the moat for?

Why were animals kept in the bailey?

Why was there a well?

Why did the bailey have a wall around it?

Activity Time

Attackers and defenders

The class will be divided into 'Attackers' and 'Defenders'. For the group you are in, do the tasks below.

DEFENDERS:

a Make a copy of the motte and bailey castle on page 33. Label it with all of the features which will help you defend the castle from attack.

b Draw and label other ways of defending your castle.

ATTACKERS:

a Make a copy of the motte and bailey castle on page 33. Label it with all of the features which will make it difficult for you to attack the castle.

b Label your drawing with ways of getting around the defences of the castle.

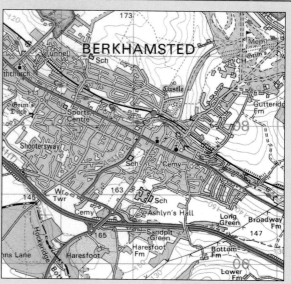
© Crown Copyright

Berkhamsted Castle

❶ Look at the modern map. What features can you see on the map which would have helped in the building of Berkhamsted Castle?

❷ Make a list of all the things that make Berkhamsted Castle easy to defend.

❸ Spot the differences between Berkhamsted Castle in Source 2 and the motte and bailey castle on page 33.

STONE CASTLES

Towards the end of his reign William and his barons built stone castles instead of wooden castles. These were called 'shell keep' castles and they were stronger than motte and bailey castles.

Question Time

1 Why do you think William and his barons started to build castles made of stone? Write down three reasons.

2 Do you think it would be easier to attack a motte and bailey castle or a stone castle? Explain why.

CONTROLLING THE LAND AND PEOPLE BY THE FEUDAL SYSTEM

In the Middle Ages there were very few rich people and many poor people. Most people lived off the land. They grew food to eat and to swap for other goods, like tools and clothes. William had conquered England in 1066. He owned all the land. This gave him great control over the country and the people. However, he could not farm all the land himself so he gave land to his barons. In return, the barons paid the king in different ways. This way of controlling land is called the feudal system.

How the feudal system worked

The barons had to promise to fight for the king and to provide knights for the king's army in return for land. The barons then gave their knights some of their land. In return, the knights promised to fight with the barons. The knights gave small areas of their land to peasants. In return, the peasants promised to farm the land.

THE FEUDAL SYSTEM

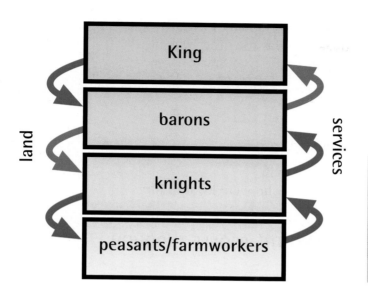

The feudal system was based on land and services. Services were providing soldiers when the king needed them or farming the land.

Activity Time

Copy out the box below and fill in the spaces. Use the diagram above and the information on page 36.

The person	What they gave	What they got
The king	Land	An army when needed
Barons	Promised to fight	
Knights	Promised to fight with their baron	
Peasants	Sometimes brought footsoldiers. Sometimes had to fight	

Question Time

The feudal system was one way in which William controlled the land and the people of England. What was the other way he controlled the land and the people?

William used land to control England by:

- keeping about one quarter for himself
- granting land as a reward to those who were loyal to him.

CONTROLLING THE LAND AND THE PEOPLE THROUGH KEEPING RECORDS

In 1085 William and his council of barons and bishops met. They decided to survey all the land of England. All land, people and animals were counted. Royal officials travelled around the country asking questions. The answers were organised into a book called the Domesday Book.

WHAT DOES THE DOMESDAY BOOK HAVE TO DO WITH CONTROL?

The Domesday Book gave William lots of information. This information helped William to know how much tax he should be able to collect. It also told him:

- how many people lived in England
- how much land and how many animals people had – this would tell him how wealthy people were, which was important for collecting taxes
- whether land had become poorer or richer between 1066 and 1086
- who held land before and after the conquest – this would tell him useful information about changes during his reign.

The Domesday Book provided William with a lot of information. It is also useful for historians today.

Activity Time

❶ Read what each of the historians wants to find out about. For one historian the Domesday Book will not give any information. Which one is it?

❷ How will the Domesday Book help other historians answer their questions?

❸ What other questions might the Domesday Book help to answer?

> *I want to find out how poor people were in the past.*

> *I want to find out what houses were made out of in the past.*

> *I want to find out how many people lived in England in the past.*

> *I want to find out how damaged England had been by the Norman Conquest.*

Activity Time

Read these two statements and decide which statement you agree with most.

Explain why you chose this one.

- *The Domesday Book shows us that William had very good control of England by 1086.*

- *The Domesday Book shows us that William did not have good control of England by 1086.*

HOW DID A SUCCESSFUL MONARCH KEEP CONTROL?

WHY WAS WILLIAM SUCCESSFUL IN CONTROLLING THE BARONS?

There were only about 12 barons in England but they were very rich and powerful and they had their own armies. They had rebelled against King Edward and it was very likely that they would rebel against William.

REWARDING THE BARONS IN 1066

William rewarded his Norman barons with the land of English barons who had been killed or had run away. English barons who had agreed to serve William were allowed to keep their land.

William also rewarded barons by making them his advisers. Two such important barons were his brother, Odo, who became Earl of Kent and William FitzOsbern who became Earl of Hereford.

I'm not going to become 'conqueror' overnight. I need 'staying power'!

Activity Time

1 How many barons were there in England?

2 Why would it be easy for the barons to rebel against a king?

3 How did William reward his Norman barons?

4 How did he reward his English barons?

5 How else did he reward barons?

6 Now write a letter from William to his brother, Odo. Expalin why you have made him Earl of Kent.

REBELLION IN 1069

In 1069 two English barons in the north of England called Edwin and Morcar rebelled against William's rule. These were the two barons who had promised to serve William at Berkhamsted. However, when William tried to get taxes from them, they changed their minds.

The rebellion was very serious because 200 Danish ships arrived in the North to join the rebel barons. The city of York was ransacked and Normans who had settled there were murdered.

William marched north and defeated the English barons and the Danes. Then he travelled around Yorkshire. He destroyed crops, animals and tools. It was winter and the peasants had no food and no way to grow more food. Thousands starved to death. This was called 'Harrying (destroying) of the North'. It took the North a very long time to recover from this destruction.

After this rebellion William changed his treatment of the barons. There were no English barons any more – they were all Norman.

SOURCE 1

In his anger at the English barons, William commanded that all crops and food should be burnt to ashes, so that the whole of the North should be stripped of all means of survival. So terrible a famine fell upon the people, that more than 100,000 young and old starved to death. My writings have often praised William, but for this act I can only condemn him.

Oderic Vitalis, writing at the time of the harrying.

CONTROL – THE OATH OF FEALTY

When William became king he insisted that his followers swear an oath of fealty (loyalty) to him. In the days when very few people could read or write and religion was important in everyone's lives, oaths were important. It was serious to break an oath.

Question Time

Look at Source 1. Oderic Vitalis was a chronicler (someone who records events in history). His mother was English and his father was French.

1 a What does Oderic say about this Harrying of the North?

b How does Oderic's own background influence his reaction to the harrying?

2 How did William control England? Choose the best answers from the list below:

- By rewarding his loyal followers.

- By paying a huge army to keep control.

- By using the feudal system.

- By finding information out about the people and land of England.

- By giving everyone the vote.

- By punishing very harshly those who rebelled.

- By making his followers swear an oath of loyalty to him.

- By making his followers sign a contract with him.

HOW SUCCESSFUL WERE ENGLISH MONARCHS IN CONTROLLING THE BOUNDARIES OF ENGLAND AND THE EMPIRE?

GETTING CONTROL OF WALES, SCOTLAND AND IRELAND

English monarchs wanted to control Wales, Scotland and Ireland for a number of reasons:

- The larger the kingdom the more powerful and rich they would be.

- They could introduce the feudal system into new areas and this would give them bigger armies.

- The more land the monarchs controlled, the more taxes they could raise.

- To stop attacks on England from Wales, Scotland and Ireland.

FRANCE

England also had an empire in France by 1200. All this land needed to be defended, particularly from the French king.

A map of the empire in 1190.

Question Time

1 a Write down the four reasons why England wanted to control Wales, Scotland and Ireland.

b Which reason tells you that English monarchs felt threatened?

2 Look at the map. William the Conqueror had been Duke of Normandy before he conquered England in 1066. By 1190 had English monarchs gained or lost land? Where was this land? Had the English monarchs been successful or failures by 1190?

THE UPS AND DOWNS OF CONTROLLING THE BORDERS

In the Activity Time boxes below and on pages 44–45 there are newsflashes about things that happened. For each one decide whether this was an up (good thing) or a down (bad thing) for medieval English monarchs. Remember the aim of the monarch was to keep control of the land around England.

Activity Time

Draw a timeline like the one shown here. You will need at least 10 centimetres for each century and 10 centimetres both above and below the line. The first one is done for you as an example.

1086 NEWS FLASH FROM WALES!
By this time Norman barons had settled in many parts of Wales.

UP

1050   1086 1100

1260 NEWS FLASH FROM WALES!
Llywelyn ap Gruffyd, ruler of Gwynedd, has united the Welsh princes.

1272 NEWS FLASH FROM WALES!
Llywelyn refuses to pay homage to (be controlled by) Edward I of England.

1276 NEWS FLASH FROM WALES!
Edward I goes to war against Llywelyn.

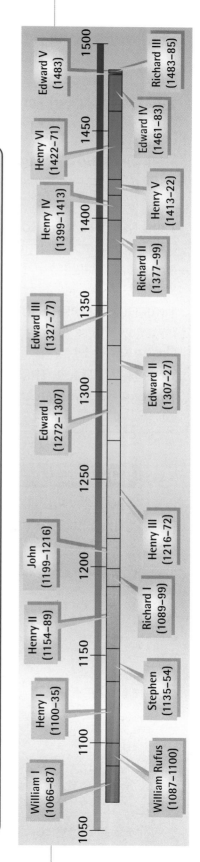

Edward V (1483)
Richard III (1483–85)
1500
Henry VI (1422–71)
Edward IV (1461–83)
1450
Henry IV (1399–1413)
Henry V (1413–22)
1400
Richard II (1377–99)
Edward III (1327–77)
1350
Edward II (1307–27)
1300
Edward I (1272–1307)
1250
Henry III (1216–72)
John (1199–1216)
1200
Richard I (1089–99)
Henry II (1154–89)
Stephen (1135–54)
1150
Henry I (1100–35)
William Rufus (1087–1100)
1100
William I (1066–87)
1050

Activity Time

Add these events to your timeline.

1282 NEWS FLASH FROM WALES!
Llywelyn and other Welsh leaders are killed.

1284 NEWS FLASH FROM WALES!
To keep Wales under control, Edward:
- *makes his son of Prince of Wales*
- *divides Wales into counties under English law and government*
- *builds seven castles.*

1399 NEWS FLASH FROM WALES!
Owain Glyndwr leads a rebellion against the English. He makes friends with the French.

1405 NEWS FLASH FROM WALES!
French soldiers land in Wales to help Owain Glyndwr.

1408 NEWS FLASH FROM WALES!
The English fight back and regain control of Wales.

Question Time

1 Look at the plan of a concentric castle.

  a What was a concentric castle? Choose the correct phrase:
- a castle with inner and outer walls
- a castle with a moat.

  b Why is a concentric castle easy to defend?

2 Look at Source 1. Apart from being a concentric castle, what else makes this castle easy to defend?

inner wall   outer wall

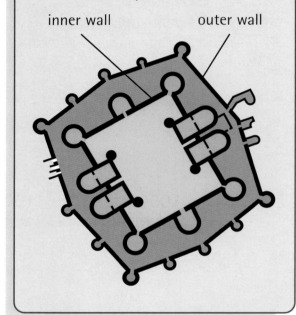

SOURCE 1

Caerphilly Castle, a concentric castle built by Edward I.

Activity Time

Now fill in the ups and downs for the English monarchs with Ireland and Scotland.

1160s NEWS FLASH FROM IRELAND!

Henry II's knights invade Ireland. Henry introduces English laws. Some English families settle in Ireland.

1390s NEWS FLASH FROM IRELAND!

Ireland is out of control. Richard II goes on two expeditions but fails to regain control.

1500 NEWS FLASH FROM IRELAND!

The English monarchs control only a small area in Ireland.

1286 NEWS FLASH FROM SCOTLAND!

Norman lords who settled in Scotland now support Scottish monarchs.

1292 NEWS FLASH FROM SCOTLAND!

Edward I defeats the Scots.

1305 NEWS FLASH FROM SCOTLAND!

William Wallace fights back against Edward I but is captured and executed.

1306 NEWS FLASH FROM SCOTLAND!

Robert Bruce is crowned King of Scotland and drives the English out.

1314 NEWS FLASH FROM SCOTLAND!

Edward II is defeated by a Scots army at the Battle of Bannockburn.

1328 NEWS FLASH FROM SCOTLAND!

Edward III accepts Bruce as King of Scotland.

Question Time

What sort of land is most likely to be conquered? Look at an atlas. What sort of land is there in Wales, Scotland and Ireland?

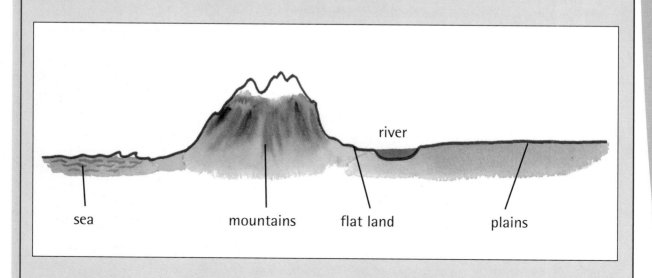

sea   mountains   flat land   plains

river

Activity Time

THE UPS AND DOWNS OF CONTROLLING THE EMPIRE

Add these events to your timeline.

1154 – Henry II controls a huge empire in France.   1154

1204 – John loses Normandy to France.   1204

1216 – The French raid England but are defeated.   1216

1294 – Edward I has only a small empire left in France.   1294

1340 – Edward III wins the Battles of Crécy and Poitiers against the French.   1340

1360 – Edward III gains control of one-third of France.   1360

1377 – The French raid the English coast.   1377

1415 – Henry V defeats the French at the Battle of Agincourt.   1415

1420 – Henry V controls half of France.   1420

1429 – Joan of Arc leads the French to victory over the English at Orleans.   1429

1453 – The English lose all their French land except Calais.   1453

Question Time

1. Study your timeline. Which medieval English monarch had the most control over the boundaries? Give two reasons for your choice.

2. Which medieval English monarch had the least control over the boundaries? Give two reasons for your choice.

3. Study the events in your timeline. For each factor listed below, select three events where this factor played an important part in helping the monarch get power and control:

   a luck **b** money **c** marriage
   d alliances (promises of help and support) **e** trouble in France.

HOW DID MEDIEVAL MONARCHS USE LAW AND ORDER AS AN INSTRUMENT OF CONTROL?

Trial by ordeal – How to find an innocent person guilty in medieval times.

①

Market day in Richmond.

② *I'm giving it away.* *It's too much.*

Will sells Edgar a foal.

③ *That foal belongs to me!*

Suddenly Edgar says it is the same foal that was stolen from him some weeks ago.

④  *The foal is mine, how do you have him? If you deny it the strength of my body and the power of justice will convict you as a liar.*

Edgar says that God is on his side.

⑤

Blessed St.Thomas Becket, help me to prove my innocence.

An ordeal by battle (a fight) is arranged between the two men for three days' time.

⑥

Will goes home to practice fighting with his brother.

⑦

Edgar and Will fight.

⑧

To everyone's surprise, Will wins.

⑨

Because Will has won it shows that God was on his side, so he is innocent.

⑩

Edgar had been lying. He confesses and is fined.

> This is a story that an historian has researched from court records of the 1170s. Medieval people thought differently from the way we think today. What is the main difference between a trial then and a trial now? What other differences are there?

THE KING WANTS CONTROL

There were three courts of law in medieval times. They were controlled by three different sets of people: the royal court was controlled by the king, the church court was controlled by the Church and the manor court was controlled by the barons. King Henry II wanted the royal court to be the most important court. However, the royal court only existed where the king happened to be.

Henry II set up a new system for the royal court. He sent travelling judges around the country to try serious crimes. He also set up the jury system.

HENRY II AND CONTROL

Henry II worked hard to keep control of the barons. He made the royal court stronger than the manor court when he could. He also wanted to make the royal court stronger than the church court. For this he was going to have to fight the Church.

Question Time

MANOR COURT	CHURCH COURT	ROYAL COURT
Under the control of barons. These were local courts in villages all over England. The barons took the money paid in fines.	Under the control of the Church. Priests were tried in church courts and they got lighter sentences than in royal courts. Some priests got away with murder!	

❶ Copy the table above. Complete it to show who controlled the royal court and what the royal court did under Henry II.

❷ Read the following crime and punishment from the Middle Ages.

Robert is guilty of stealing a deer from the Royal Forest. He is 12 years old, so he counts as an adult. He is executed by hanging.

a Find at least two things about this crime and punishment that are different from crime and punishment today.

b If Robert had stolen his neighbour's pig, his arm would have been cut off. What else does this tell you about how medieval people thought about crime and punishment?

CHURCH OR STATE – WHO WAS IN CONTROL?

We are going to use different stories from the Middle Ages to help answer the question: **How did medieval monarchs keep control?**

The story of Henry II and Thomas Becket tells us a great deal about the fight for control between the king and the Church in the Middle Ages. Here are some different accounts.

SOURCE 1

A painting from about 1200 showing the murder of Thomas Becket.

SOURCE 2

December 1170: Becket dead!
According to an eyewitness, a monk called Edward Grim, this is what happened in the cathedral:

The murderers came in full armour, with swords and axes ... they called out. 'Where is Thomas Becket, traitor to the king and to the country?' At this Becket came down the steps and answered, 'Here I am'...

'You shall die this instant!' they cried.

Becket lowered his head as if he was praying. The wicked knight leapt suddenly upon him and wounded him in the head.

Next he received a second blow on the head, but still he stood firm.

At the third blow he fell on his knees and elbows, saying in a low voice, 'For the name of Jesus I am ready to die.'

The next blow took off the top of his head and the blood stained the floor.

Question Time

Use Source 2. Write one sentence to answer the question 'Why did Becket die?'

SOURCE 3

July – December 1170: going back in time

Becket had promised Henry that he would obey Henry instead of the Pope. But in 1170 he broke his promise and expelled (excommunicated) from the Church all the bishops who supported Henry. Being excommunicated was very serious because you could not take mass and you would go to hell. Henry was so angry when he heard this that he shouted out: 'Who will rid me of this troublesome priest?' Some of Henry's knights heard what he said and went off to kill Becket. When Henry realised the knights had gone, he tried to stop them but it was too late.

Question Time

Use Source 3. Write one sentence to answer the question 'Why did Becket die?'

SOURCE 4

1164–70: rewinding the story

Becket was a long-standing friend of Henry. But when Becket became Archbishop of Canterbury, he supported the Pope and the Church instead of Henry.

When Henry passed a law saying that all serious crimes should be tried in the royal court and not in the church court, Becket did not support him. Becket saw quite clearly that Henry wanted to have more control over the church courts.

In 1170, Henry II asked the Archbishop of York to crown his son as the future king. Usually the Archbishop of Canterbury did this and so this was an insult to Becket.

Question Time

Use Source 4. Write one sentence to answer the question 'Why did Becket die?'

SOURCE 5

1154–64: back to the beginning

In 1154 Henry became King of England. He asked his friend Thomas Becket to be his adviser. At first the two men worked well together.

Henry wanted to increase his power over the Church in England (taking power away from the Pope):

- *He wanted to appoint his own men to be bishops.*

- *He wanted to control the church courts. This is because priests and bishops who were accused of committing serious crimes like murder were tried in the church courts. Punishments were much lighter than in the royal courts. Henry wanted to stop this happening.*

In 1162 Henry made Becket Archbishop of Canterbury. He thought Becket would help him.

Question Time

1 Use Source 5. Write one sentence to answer the question 'Why did Becket die?'

2 Look at your answers to the questions on Sources 2 to 5. Then answer true or false to the following statement.

As the story of Henry II and Becket moves back in time, it has more to do with a power struggle between the king and the Church than a personal quarrel.

THE STRUGGLE BETWEEN KING AND CHURCH

The Church was very important in people's lives. Everyone went to church on a Sunday. There were churches in villages and towns all over England.

WHY DID BECKET DIE?

Two historians are studying the death of Becket. They are arguing about the reasons for it.

A Becket died because of a personal quarrel between himself and Henry II. The two men had been friends but they fell out. When Henry got really angry he told his knights to kill Becket.

B Becket died because of a power struggle over who controlled the Church. Henry II thought that he, and not the Pope, should control the English Church.

Question Time

Look at Source 4.

❶ Why did Henry want serious crimes tried in the king's court?

❷ Which historian's argument does this support (A or B)?

WHAT HAPPENED WHEN MONARCHS LOST CONTROL?

KING JOHN

Some kings were not very good at keeping control. One of these was King John.

In June 1215, King John fled from London. The barons were very angry about the way he was treating them and they were marching to London to confront John. John knew that he could not defeat the barons and so he agreed to meet them.

SOURCE 1

A picture of King John, taken from a fourteenth-century manuscript.

KING JOHN MEETS THE BARONS

On 15 June King John met the barons in a meadow called Runnymede, near the River Thames. King John had to agree to the demands made by the barons. These were written down and called the Magna Carta or Great Charter. This was the first time that a king was forced to obey rules. King John had lost control.

WHY HAD KING JOHN LOST CONTROL?

There were a number of reasons why King John lost control.

John demanded heavier taxes than ever before from his barons. Sometimes, if they refused to pay, he hanged their sons.

King John fought the French king but still lost Normandy. In the eyes of the English barons he was a failure as a warrior.

John quarrelled with the Pope over who should choose the Archbishop of Canterbury. The Pope was so angry he banned all church services in England. This meant that English people could not be christened, go to church for mass or have a Christian burial.

John's brother, Richard I, had spent a great deal of money fighting in France and in the Crusades. This meant John was poor when he became king.

DEATH OF KING JOHN

In 1216, a year after signing the Magna Carta, John died.

Question Time

Read the section headed 'Why had King John lost control?'

1 Why was John poor when he became king?

2 Write down two reasons why the barons were angry with King John.

3 Why did the barons think that John was a failure?

4 Why did John quarrel with the Pope?

5 a Why was the Pope's ban on church services so terrible for English people?

b What does this tell you about the way in which medieval English people thought?

The main points of the Magna Carta

• *Taxes could not be increased without the permission of the barons and the bishops.*

• *Freemen could not be put in prison without a fair trial.*

• *The king could not appoint his own men to be bishops and archbishops.*

• *Barons had to pay only £100 to inherit land, not the huge sums John had demanded.*

Why the barons wrote the Magna Carta

The Magna Carta only applied to freemen such as the barons. A freeman was a person who owned land and property. Most people did not actually own land, they were allowed to farm only on land given to them in return for work. These people were not free.

Over time more people became free so the Magna Carta became more important.

Question Time

Read the sections on this page about the Magna Carta.

1 Which groups of people did the Magna Carta apply to?

2 Very few people were free. What did this mean?

3 Why did the Magna Carta become more important later?

4 Which point of the Magna Carta is still very important today?

WAS KING JOHN IN CONTROL?

Some historians argue that John was a bad king. They say:

- In 1213 John gave up some power to the Pope.
- In 1214 John was defeated by the French.
- In 1215 the barons forced John to sign the Magna Carta.
- In 1216 John died with little money and the French had taken over London.

Activity Time

Here are two groups of evidence: Evidence Group A and Evidence Group B. Find a partner. One of you will read Group A and the other one will read Group B. As you read, ask yourself the question: **How bad a king was John?**

Evidence Group A

SOURCE 1

Hell itself is made more horrible by the foulness of King John.

Matthew Paris, writing in the thirteenth century.

SOURCE 2

John was a tyrant. He lost Normandy and many other lands.

Matthew Paris, writing in the thirteenth century.

SOURCE 4

Geoffrey, a priest, said it was not safe for priests to work for John. John heard of this and put him in prison, dressed him in lead and starved him to death.

Roger of Wendover, writing in the thirteenth century.

SOURCE 3

John – a faithless son, a treacherous brother ... broke every promise.

Quoted in Stubbs' *Constitutional History* **in 1875.**

Evidence Group B

SOURCE 1

John made sure that justice was done in the courts. He was merciful to widows, orphans and poor people who had done wrong.

From a history textbook, written in the 1960s.

SOURCE 2

John was generous ... to outsiders. He trusted English people less than he trusted foreigners, so they abandoned him.

From the *Barnwell Chronicle.*

SOURCE 3

If anyone harms the Jews in your city, always protect them.

John's orders to an English city.

Question Time

1 The person who is reading Evidence Group A should complete the following sentence.

King John was a bad king because he

_____

The person who is reading Evidence Group B should complete the following sentence.

King John was not a bad king because he

_____

2 Why are your answers so different?

3 Answer true or false to the following statement:

An historian needs to read as many different sources as possible to get the most accurate picture of the past.

4 Matthew Paris and Roger of Wendover were both monks. Look back to page 54. Why do you think that they might not like King John?

5 Stubbs based his book on the evidence of Matthew Paris and Roger of Wendover. How does this help us to understand what Stubbs says about King John?

SOURCE 4

John was well-educated, intelligent and active in governing his kingdom. In these ways John was a better ruler than his brother, Richard I. But Richard was admired for his successes on the battlefield and John suffered heavy defeats.

An extract from a modern history textbook.

CONTROLLING THE SUCCESSION: COULD WOMEN RULE?

All the monarchs between 1066 and 1500 were men. Most medieval people did not think that a woman could rule.

WHO WAS MATILDA?

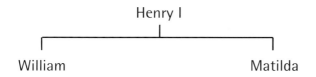

```
              Henry I
        ┌───────┴───────┐
     William          Matilda
```

At the age of 12, Matilda was sent by her father, Henry I, to Germany. She was to marry Henry V, the Holy Roman Emperor. This marriage would make Henry I and England more powerful. Matilda's husband died and her father chose another husband for her even though she was 24 years old and against the marriage.

MATILDA'S BROTHER DIES

In 1120, William was drowned at sea. William was Henry's only son, so he was heir to the English throne. The big question now was: who would rule England after the death of Henry I?

MATILDA AND STEPHEN

Both Matilda and her cousin Stephen had a claim to the throne.

Matilda was the daughter of King Henry I. She understood about power and control.

Stephen was the nephew of King Henry I. He had the support of some powerful barons.

SOURCE 1

A picture of Matilda from a medieval manuscript.

SOURCE 2

Matilda sent for the richest men and demanded a huge sum of money. They complained that they did not have any money left because of the war. When they said this, Matilda, every trace of a woman's gentleness removed from her face, blazed into unbearable fury.

From *Gesta Stephani*. The author wrote this book to make people support Stephen.

THE NEED FOR THE BARONS' SUPPORT

Some of the barons did not want a woman to rule England. However, Henry decided to make Matilda his heir and he made all the barons promise to support her. Some kept their promise but others did not. Henry died soon after, in 1135, and Matilda became queen. This led to civil war.

CIVIL WAR

In 1141 Matilda defeated Stephen but he soon escaped and started fighting again. In the end Matilda gave up. However, Stephen had no children. Matilda made him promise that her son Henry would be the next king.

We can build all the castles we want. The king is too busy fighting to care.

It's just the same when Matilda is winning. The civil war gives us a chance to increase our power.

Barons talking during the civil war.

SOURCE 3

Just about this time (1141) Stephen's wife, a woman with the determination of a man, sent messengers to Matilda. The messengers asked Matilda to free Stephen from his filthy dungeon...But Matilda shouted at them in harsh and insulting language.

The people of London were in big trouble now. Their land was being destroyed by the war. This new lady was going too far. So the whole city took up weapons against Matilda. She was just about to eat a well-cooked feast. But on hearing the noises from the city, she and all her followers ran away.

From *Gesta Stephani.*

Question Time

1. Who was Matilda?

2. Did Matilda have any choice about the person she married? What sort of husband did a king want his daughter to have?

3. Read Sources 2 and 3. What do you learn from this source about how women were supposed to behave in medieval times?

4. How did some barons take advantage of the civil war?

WHAT CHALLENGES DID MEDIEVAL MONARCHS FACE?

You have learned about the ways in which the medieval monarchs of England kept control and what happened if they lost it.

Activity Time

1 You are a medieval monarch. Here are some of your problems. Match the answers to the problems.

Problems	Answers
Some of the English barons do not want you as monarch	Get information about everyone in England so you can tax them.
A Welsh prince leads a rebellion.	Grant land to loyal barons. Punish the disloyal barons.
Scots raid the borders.	Marry a Danish princess.
Barons want more power and the right to agree to taxation.	Fight the Welsh and build royal castles to keep the Welsh down.
The Danish threaten to attack.	Make an agreement with the Pope's enemy
The Pope and archbishops want to be powerful.	Fight the Scots and suggest your daughter marries a Scottish prince.
Need money to fight wars and to run the country.	Be successful in war. Don't ask for too many taxes. Keep your royal castles strong.

2 You are worried about your son's health. If he dies then your daughter will be queen. What extra problems does she face? What advice would you give her?

Unit 3: How hard was life for medieval people in town and country?

Life was very hard for most people. Many people worked like slaves on land belonging to rich people. A bad harvest or flooding could cause many people to starve.

WHAT DID MEDIEVAL ENGLAND LOOK LIKE?

Villages

Most villages were made up of peasants' houses, a church, a manor house and a mill. The person who owned all the land in the village lived in the manor. There were large fields around each village. Barley and wheat were grown for food. Villagers kept pigs and sheep, which grazed on the wasteland around the village. This wasteland was not good enough for growing crops and the peasants shared it for grazing animals.

Towns

A few people lived in towns. Towns were places to buy and sell goods. Many towns had walls around them and gates which were closed at night to protect the town.

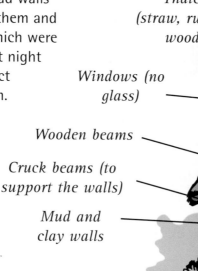

An artist's reconstruction of a peasant house.

Fire in centre of house – no chimney

Thatched roof (straw, rushes, turf or wooden tiles)

Windows (no glass)

Wooden beams

Cruck beams (to support the walls)

Mud and clay walls

One or two rooms, often shared with animals

WHAT DOES THE DOMESDAY BOOK TELL US ABOUT LIFE IN TOWN AND COUNTRY?

The Domesday Book is one of the most important documents for finding out about medieval life. It was written in 1086. William the Conqueror wanted information about people in England. This was so that he could tax people.

William's officials travelled around England asking questions about all the land, animals and people.

How many mills are there?

How many ploughs are there?

How much woodland is there?

How many hides are there?

How many pigs are there?

SOURCE 1

There was not a single 'hide' of land, not even one ox, nor one cow, nor one pig which escaped notice.

From the Anglo-Saxon Chronicle, written in the eleventh century.

PEOPLE IN THE DOMESDAY BOOK

In the Middle Ages people were organised into different levels. Each level of person had a different label which the Domesday Book used:

- **Lords** were the king, barons, knights or churchmen who owned land. Other people, lower in status, would work on this land. The lord would keep some land for growing food for himself. This piece of land was called the demesne.
- A **reeve** was a man who looked after the lord's land for him.
- **Freemen** paid rent to the lord and did some work for him. They were free to come and go.
- **Villeins** were granted land but had to work for the lord. They could not leave the manor without the lord's permission.
- **Bordars** and **cottars** were often poorer than villeins but were free.
- **Slaves** had no land. They worked for the lord.

Question Time

1. Read Source 1. What was a hide?

2. Which peasants were not free?

3. Historians have used the Domesday Book to work out how many people were freemen, villeins, bordars, cottars, slaves, reeves and lords. They can also work out how much land was held by them. These are the figures in the yellow box. Copy the pie chart. Colour it in using a different colour for each section of land. Then label the pie chart with who held what land. One section has been done for you. Who holds no land? Who holds most land, considering there are only a few of them?

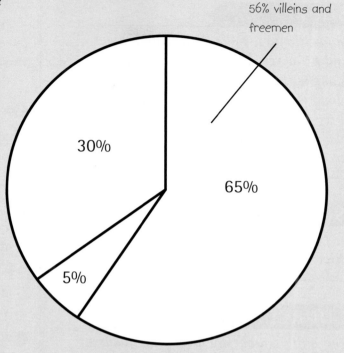

56% villeins and freemen

30%

65%

5%

	Per cent of population	Per cent of land
Slaves	9	No land
Bordars/cottars	32	5
Villeins/freemen	56	65
King, barons, church	3	30

LAND IN THE DOMESDAY BOOK

There are different words for land as well as for people in the Domesday Book.

Manor Large farm belonging to a lord.	**Demesne** Part of the manor that produced food for the lord and his family.	**Hide** A piece of land measuring 120 acres, or 50 hectares.	**Ploughs** A measurement of how rich the land was. More ploughs showed there was more land that was rich enough to grow crops on.

Here are some extracts from the Domesday Book.

SOURCE 2

In Wallington, Fulco holds three hides and 40 acres. There is land for five ploughs. In demesne there are two ploughs. There are four villeins with three ploughs. The three bordars have two ploughs. There is one cottar and two slaves.

SOURCE 3

In Lambeth there is woodland with three pigs.

SOURCE 4

The mill at Stokesay gives nine loads of corn. There is a miller.

SOURCE 5

At Alveston there is a fishery with 1300 eels.

SOURCE 6

The manor of Ilford paid 16,000 herrings to the lord William of Warenne every year.

SOURCE 7

Bury town includes land which is ploughed and sown. Altogether there are 30 priests and 28 nuns who say prayers daily. There are 75 millers, ale-brewers, tailors, washerwomen, shoemakers, robe-makers, cooks, carriers, dispensers. There are 13 reeves and 22 bordars under them.

Question Time

1 Make a glossary of these medieval words:

reeve, villein, freeman, bordars and cottars, slaves, manor, demesne, hide. You will find meanings for the words on pages 62 and 63.

2 Read Source 2.

a What is the name of the lord who holds Wallington?

b How big is his manor? (The manor is all the land he holds.)

c How many ploughs are needed for the lord's part of the manor of Wallington?

d Who are the poorest people in Wallington?

3 Read all the sources. According to these parts of the Domesday Book, what different types of food were eaten in medieval England?

4 Read Source 7 and compare it to Sources 2–6. In what ways was a town different from a manor in the country? In what ways was a town similar to a manor?

5 It is 1087. William Rufus is the new king. He wants to know how much tax he can get from the English. You are one of his advisers. You suggest he can put a tax on all sorts of things. Role play a scene where you show him the Domesday Book and tell him why it is useful to him. He may ask you how reliable it is. You can reply that his father sent two separate sets of officials to ask questions at different times. A number of people were questioned in every village.

WAS LIFE ALWAYS HARD FOR MEDIEVAL PEASANTS? HOW CAN WE FIND OUT?

The Domesday Book does not tell us everything about medieval life. Think of one thing it does not tell you about.

To find out more, we need to use other sources of information.

SOURCE 1

One photograph shows the medieval method of strip farming. The other shows the enclosed fields of modern farming.

MEDIEVAL AND MODERN FARMERS

Farming was different in the Middle Ages.

In medieval times, fields were 'open'. This means they did not have hedges or fences. Each field was divided into strips. Each peasant farmed a few strips of each field.

One of the open fields would always be left fallow. This means that no crops would be grown on it. This allowed the soil to rest and get back the goodness it lost when crops grew on it. The other two fields would grow crops like wheat and barley.

SOURCE 2

English peasants had short hair, shaved beards and golden bracelets. They drank too much ale.

William of Malmesbury, writing in the eleventh century.

SOURCE 3

Every village had a blacksmith, a carpenter and others with special jobs. The only essential goods brought in from outside were salt and iron. Otherwise each village could support itself.

Description of a medieval village by a modern historian in 1972.

SOURCE 4

This picture from the Luttrell Psalter shows peasants reaping and binding corn into sheaves.

SOURCE 5

I have no pennies to buy pullets,
Nor geese nor pigs, but I have two green cheeses,
A few curds of cream, a cake of oatmeal,
Two loaves of beans and bran, baked for my children,
But I have parsley and pot herbs and plenty of cabbages,
And a cow and calf.
This is the little we must live on till the Lammas season.

An extract from the poem *Piers Plowman* by William Langland, written in the fourteenth century.

SOURCE 6

In the manor of Borley, Essex, peasants' services for the lord: three days' work each week ploughing, carrying manure, weeding, mowing the meadow and reaping.

Manor Court records, from the fourteenth century.

Question Time

1 Read Source 3. What were the only essential goods brought in from outside?

2 Read Source 5. Make a list of the food that the family had to last until the Lammas season.

3 Look at Sources 2–6. In what ways was life hard for medieval peasants?

A medieval picture of Boarstall, a small medieval village.

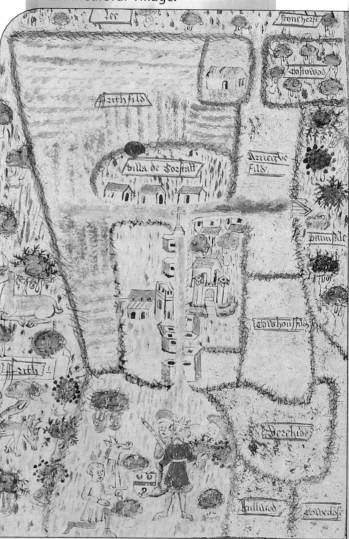

Activity Time

1 Look at Source 7. Make a sketch of the village. Label the following on your sketch: church, peasant houses, fields (with strips), woodland, demesne (lord's house and land), main street. Can you find a mill?

2 We find information from different sources. Write out the sentences below matching each statement to its source.

Statement	Source
In the village of Gelly there was enough land for six ploughs.	We know this from archaelogy.
The peasants who were villeins had to do three days' work each week – ploughing, weeding and harvesting.	This is from the Domesday Book.
They were so poor that they could hardly feed their children.	We know this from manor court records.
Only two buildings in the village were made of stone.	We know this from poetry.

WAS LIFE ANY BETTER IN A MEDIEVAL TOWN?

THE GROWTH OF TOWNS

The Domesday Book named just over 100 small towns. Very few had more than 10,000 people living in them. Towns changed in the Middle Ages. They grew larger and there were more of them.

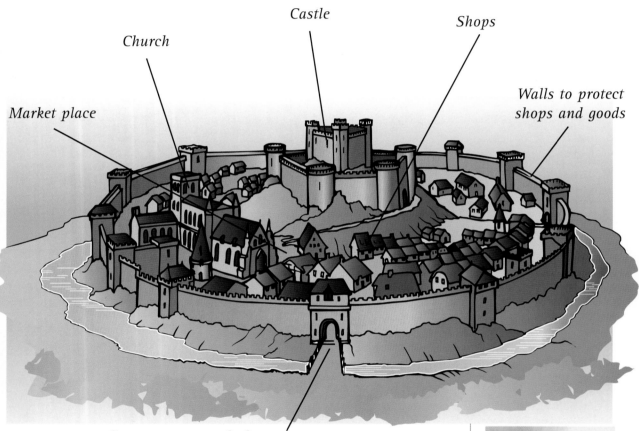

Castle

Shops

Church

Walls to protect shops and goods

Market place

Strangers were asked questions about why they were visiting the town. The gates were shut at night.

An artist's drawing of Salisbury in the Middle Ages.

BUYING AND SELLING IN TOWNS

There were markets in the towns. Peasants came from the surrounding countryside with food to sell. They would exchange this for things like woollen cloth and iron pans.

There were shops such as shoemakers, tailors, bakers, butchers and ale-makers.

PROTECTING THE TOWN

Towns usually had walls to protect the shops and goods belonging to the traders. There was a gate in the wall that was closed at sunset. Outsiders coming to the town were questioned about why they had come to the town.

PEOPLE IN THE TOWN

Peasant: I come from a village five miles away, to sell my butter and cheese.

Town dweller: I'm a shoemaker and have lived and worked in the town all my life.

Merchant: I come to the town to trade in cloth.

Villein: I ran away from my lord's manor a year and a day ago. I have supported myself and paid taxes. This means I am now free and my lord cannot force me to go back to the manor.

Question Time

1 Write down the reason why each of the talking heads is in the town.

2 Spot the differences between a medieval town and a village. How many can you find?

WHAT WERE MEDIEVAL TOWNS LIKE?

Medieval towns had narrow streets. They were noisy, crowded and dirty. People emptied all their waste (including toilet waste) into the street. The houses on each side of the streets were often shops. The shopkeepers made their goods in the back rooms and sold them in their shops at the front. Sometimes the streets were called after the craftsmen in them, such as Baker Street. Streets where butchers lived and worked were often called The Shambles because of the mess of meat, bones and fat thrown into the middle of the roadway. There were no sewers, no running water, no rubbish collection and nobody cleaned the streets.

TOWN GUILDS

Guilds were groups of craftsmen with their own rules (for example carpenters, weavers and shoemakers). These people got together to protect their craft.

ENTERTAINMENT

Guilds also organised entertainment such as plays and feasts. Most towns had a fair once a year. As well as goods to buy and sell, there would be jugglers, wrestling matches and puppet shows.

Activity Time

❶ Below is a drawing of the medieval town on page 68. Sketch this leaving plenty of space for labels. Label your drawing with as much information about towns as you can find on pages 68, 69 and 70.

❷ Find out more about one area of medieval life in a town. Choose from the list below.

- How clean were medieval towns?
- How safe were medieval towns?
- How did people make money?
- What were buildings like?

WHY DID TOWNS GROW IN THE MIDDLE AGES?

During the Middle Ages the number of towns in Britain doubled. Many of the towns that existed in the eleventh century were much bigger by the fourteenth century. This was because there was more trade. There was more trade because:

- Manors were growing more food. The peasants sold the extra food in the town market. This gave them more money to spend on things like shoes, iron pans and ale. Traders had more money. There were more traders in the towns and they built more houses to live in.

- Barons built castles. All the people building and living in the castle had to buy food and other goods.

- Many sheep were kept in England in the Middle Ages, so wool was traded in the towns. Traders and townspeople had money to spend.

Question Time

Copy the chart below. Fill in the blanks to show the reasons why towns grew.

Three reasons why towns grew in the Middle Ages

Manors grew extra food	Peasants sold extra food in the town market	Towns grew because there were more shops and markets
	Castle people bought food and other goods	Towns grew because …
Many sheep were kept in England		Towns grew because of the wool trade

Activity Time

Get into pairs. One of you is a town dweller. You have a market stall selling woollen cloth. You are poor, but you hope to make more and more money as the town grows.

One of you is a villein who lives in a village. You do not like being obedient to your lord. You are thinking of running away to the town.

Each of you must then:

1 Make a list of things you like about the way you live.

2 Make a list of things you do not like about the way you live.

3 Have a conversation about whether the villein should move to the town or not.

WHY WAS THE BLACK DEATH SO TERRIFYING?

Look carefully at Source 1. What is shown in the picture? What is each figure doing? What does it mean? Why do you think a picture like this might be put in a stained glass window of the church?

THE WAY WE LOOK AT DEATH TODAY

Science has shaped the way in which we look at death today. We know:

- more about the causes of illnesses and deaths

- that germs can be passed from one person to another and spread disease

- that each person has an immune system which fights illness

- that people can sometimes become immune to diseases which they have been in contact with.

THE WAY THEY LOOKED AT DEATH IN THE MIDDLE AGES

In the Middle Ages people did not have the scientific knowledge that we have today. The Church taught that God was responsible for everything that happened. If bad things happened it was because God was angry with you.

SOURCE 1

An image of death in a sixteenth-century stained glass window.

THE BLACK DEATH OF 1349

The plague known as the Black Death spread across Europe and reached England in 1348. The first cases were at a small port called Melcombe Regis in Dorset. In 1349 it spread very quickly to all parts of England, Wales and Scotland.

SOURCE 2

Bodies being buried during the Black Death.

THE SYMPTOMS AND TREATMENT

The symptoms could include huge swellings in the armpits. There could be black patches on the skin. Some people vomited blood. People died within three or four days.

Some people tried medicines such as herbs, vinegar or parts of dead animals. But these treatments did not work because people did not understand how the plague spread.

FLEAS, RATS AND SHIPS

The plague was spread by fleas that lived on black rats. The black rats came to England on ships. They left the ships and lived in the dirty, crowded towns.

SO MANY DEAD

Many people died. The graveyards of large towns like London quickly filled up. Trench diggers were paid a lot of money to dig mass graves. In the country, dead bodies could be seen in the fields and by the road.

THE RETURN OF THE PLAGUE

The Black Death of 1349 was followed by another bad outbreak of plague in 1361. This was known as the children's plague because more children died than adults. The plague kept on returning until 1666.

Question Time

1 What were the symptoms of the plague?

2 Why do you think it was called the Black Death?

3 a What sort of medicines did people try?

   b Why did the medicines not work?

HOW MANY PEOPLE DIED?

We do not know how many people died from the Black Death. In the Middle Ages there were no records of population figures. Historians think that about a third of the population died from the Black Death. This means that the number of people living in Britain fell from about 3.5 million in 1348 to about 2.5 million by 1500.

SOURCE 4

Lincolnshire and the Black Death

Over 100 deserted villages have been discovered.

Church records tell us that 40 per cent of the clergy died.

SOURCE 3

An aerial photograph of a village deserted during the Black Death. Outlines of buildings and fields can still be seen.

WHAT DID PEOPLE THINK CAUSED THE PLAGUE?

Many people thought that God was angry. They thought that he sent the plague as a punishment for people being bad. Some people prayed. Some people whipped themselves to show they were sorry for their sins. They hoped this would stop the plague spreading.

Some people had crazy ideas about the cause of the plague. They thought that Jewish people had poisoned the water. In some places in Europe, Jews were murdered.

Some people thought that the plague was caused by dirty air. Human waste was cleaned from the streets.

In fact, the plague was spread by rats! Tiny fleas, living on the rats, would pass the disease on to humans. The rats came to Britain on ships from all over Europe.

Question Time

True or False?

Aerial photographs can help historians to work out how many people died in the Black Death.

Question Time

Look at the boxes below. On the left are reasons that medieval people gave as causes for the plague. On the right are descriptions of what medieval people thought.

Reasons for plague	What/how medieval people thought	What they did to solve the problem
God is angry	God sent the plague as a punishment for people being bad.	
Jewish people	Some people thought Jewish people had poisoned the water.	
Dirty/bad air	Some people thought that the plague was caused by dirty air as shown by the smell from all the waste in the streets.	

1 Read the paragraph headed 'What did people think caused the plague?' Fill in the third column by describing what they did to solve the problem.

2 Which of the three solutions might have helped? Give a reason for your answer.

Activity Time

A Causes and Results

Read the statements below. Decide which statements tell you about **causes** of the Black Death and which tell you about **results** of the Black Death.

Head your page **The Black Death**. Divide your page in half. Head one column **Causes** and the other column **Results**. Copy out the statements putting each one in the correct column.

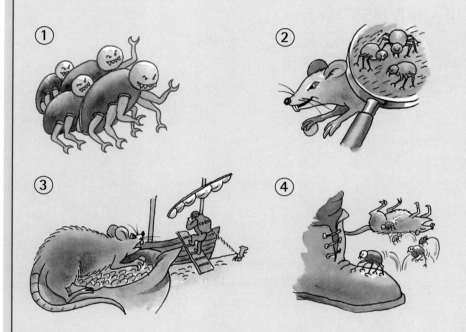

How rats spread the plague.

The plague came into England on ships from Europe.

Most people died very quickly, within three or four days.

The plague was carried by fleas on the black rat.

Some people blamed the Jews for the plague.

The population of Britain and Europe decreased because of the plague. About one third of the people died.

Whole villages were abandoned because of the plague.

Some people thought God had sent the plague.

The Black Death was a turning point in history in the Middle Ages. This is because it changed life dramatically.

MORE AND MORE PEOPLE IN THE MIDDLE AGES

For hundreds of years the population of Britain was growing. This meant that there were more and more mouths to feed. By 1300 nearly all the good land in England was being farmed. Yet the population kept on growing. In 1315, there was a bad famine and many people died. Even in good years there was not enough food to keep everyone strong and healthy. Some historians think that the Black Death was a disaster waiting to happen.

WAS THE BLACK DEATH A DISASTER?

The Black Death was not a disaster for the people who survived. There were fewer people. Suddenly there was:

- more food to go round

- more land to go round

- fewer workers to farm the land, so workers could ask for higher wages.

I need workers to farm my land.

There are a lot of us workers around. I'm lucky to get work. I'll work for 2 pence a day.

There aren't enough of us workers around. That lord will be lucky to have me. I want to be paid 5 pence a day.

Question Time

Look at the cartoon picture on page 78.

1 **a** Is the large group showing peasants before or after 1349?

b Is the small group showing peasants before or after 1349?

c Which group will be paid the higher wages?

d Look at the sentences opposite. Write out the correct sentence that tells you why one of the groups will be paid higher wages.

2 Read page 78. Why do you think some historians think that the Black Death was a disaster waiting to happen?

> **Higher Wages**
>
> *The large group will be paid higher wages because there are more of them.*
>
> *The large group will be paid higher wages because more food is needed.*
>
> *The small group will be paid higher wages because they like their lord.*
>
> *The large group will be paid higher wages because they are not greedy.*
>
> *The small group will be paid higher wages because there are not enough workers around.*

WHY WAS THERE A PEASANTS' REVOLT IN 1381?

In medieval times, people were supposed to know their place and to stay there. Very few peasants ever became knights and very few knights ever became barons.

However, the Black Death of 1349 had given peasants more power than they had had before:

- They could demand higher wages to work on the lord's land.

- Many unfree peasants (villeins and slaves) were able to buy their freedom.

- The peasants were less willing to be told what to do by their lords.

A painting showing Richard II meeting Wat Tyler in 1381.

THE PEASANTS' REVOLT

Look at Source 1. The man in the picture wearing a crown is King Richard II. He was 14 years old. The man on his left wearing a grey hat is Wat Tyler. Wat Tyler was the leader of the Peasants' Revolt.

The picture shows two events. It is like a cartoon without a line down the middle. The left side happened first. It shows Richard II meeting Wat Tyler. Wat Tyler asked the king for some changes. Tyler was then murdered by the Mayor of London. The right side happened next. Richard spoke to the crowd of peasants. We know from other sources that most of them did not have armour. This is just how the artist decided to paint them.

CAUSES OF THE PEASANTS' REVOLT

Historians organise causes into two different groups. Long-term causes are things that have been going on for a long time. Short-term causes are things that happen just before the big event. Below are some long-term and short-term causes of the Peasants' Revolt.

Richard II's advisers gave bad advice about how to treat people.

Young king, bad advice

In 1351 a law was passed fixing the maximum wage a peasant could be paid.

Keeping wages down

The war with France was going badly from 1369.

Losing war

The king needed money for the war. In 1377 and 1379 Poll Taxes were demanded. Everyone over the age of 15 had to pay a tax.

First and second Poll Taxes

Some priests went around saying that all men were equal to each other.

New ideas

In 1381, a third Poll Tax was demanded. Some of the peasants revolted.

Third Poll Tax 1381

Many peasants wanted more money and freedom after the Black Death.

Peasants more powerful

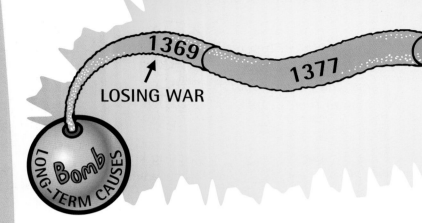

LOSING WAR

LONG-TERM CAUSES Bomb

1369 1377 1379

Activity Time

❶ Copy out the drawing above, leaving room to write above and below. Look at the talking heads on page 81. Above the fuse, fill in the headings written under the correct talking heads. The first one is done for you.

❷ Under the bomb, write a list of the long-term causes of the Peasants' Revolt. Again just use the headings from the talking heads.

❸ On top of the flame write down the event that made the peasants' anger explode in 1381.

WAS THE REVOLT SUCCESSFUL?

Richard II's conversation with the peasants went something like this:

Wat Tyler: We have two demands – all villeins must be free and rent for land must be fixed at 2d per acre.

Richard II: I agree to your demands.

Then Wat Tyler was killed. Richard spoke to the peasants.

Richard II: I agree to your demands. I promise. Now go home.

THE PEASANTS GO HOME

The peasants did go home but Richard II broke his promise to them. He did not give them their demands. Soldiers were sent to arrest any peasants still in London. Then more soldiers were sent to capture the leaders of the revolt. They were hanged and their bodies were left hanging as a warning to others. The priest who had preached that all men were equal was also hanged.

THE POLL TAX

Poll is an old-fashioned word for head. A Poll Tax is a tax on every single person. It is always a hated tax. A Poll Tax was introduced in England and Wales in 1990. There were riots and many people would not pay. In the end the Poll Tax was abolished. People preferred to pay tax in other ways such as income tax, VAT, council tax, or capital gains tax.

Question Time

Put the sentences below in chronological order (the order in which they happened).

- Richard II told the peasants that he agreed to their demands.

- Wat Tyler was murdered.

- In 1377 and 1379 Poll Taxes were introduced.

- The young king, Richard II rode to meet Wat Tyler and the peasants.

- Richard II broke his promise to the peasants.

- In 1381 the third Poll Tax was introduced and Wat Tyler led a Peasants' Revolt to march on London.

HOW HARD WAS LIFE FOR MEDIEVAL PEOPLE IN TOWN AND COUNTRY?

FILMS AND TELEVISION STORIES ABOUT MEDIEVAL BRITAIN

Many films and television stories have been made about medieval Britain.

These films can help us picture what medieval Britain looked like. But sometimes these films are not historically accurate. This means they do not show medieval Britain as it really was.

Look at Source 1 on page 84. In what ways is it not an accurate picture of medieval life? Why do you think filmmakers might not want to show medieval life accurately?

A still from the 1995 film, *First Knight*.

Activity Time

You are a researcher for a Hollywood film company. Your director is making a film set in medieval England and sends you a questionnaire to copy out and fill in.

Letter from the Director to the Researcher

Dear Researcher,

Please could you fill in the answers to the questionnaire. We are making a film about a villein who lives in a medieval village. He has to work on his lord's demesne as well as farming his own strips in the open fields. He decides to run away to the town so that he can be free. The town he runs to is Canterbury. There he sees the great Archbishop of Canterbury who was later murdered on the orders of the king. We might bring in a bit about the Black Death just for some extra drama.

Can you fill me in on the details? Please fill in the questionnaire with as much information as you can.

From the Director.

Questionnaire

1 What is a villein?

2 What is the demesne?

3 What were open fields?
   Were they bigger than fields today?

4 How long does the villein have to hide in the town before he can be free?

5 What was the name of the Archbishop of Canterbury?

6 What was the name of the king who brought about his murder?

7 I know the Black Death was in 1349. What caused the Black Death?

8 When was Becket's murder?
   Why was he murdered?

Unit 4: How did the medieval church affect people's lives?

WHY HAVE SO MANY MEDIEVAL CHURCHES SURVIVED UNTIL TODAY?

SOURCE 1

This is a modern aerial photograph of the city of Durham. You could scan the photograph and remove the modern buildings and bridges. Probably the cathedral and the castle will be the only medieval buildings left. Can you see any other buildings that might be medieval? Can you answer the questions below?

Find the cathedral.

Find the castle.

What would the medieval houses be made from?

What does the cathedral tell you about power?

What would the cathedral and castle be made from?

Why was this place chosen for a castle?

Why do you think people built the cathedral to last for longer than their houses?

WHAT WAS THE CHURCH?

In the Middle Ages, almost everyone in England was Christian. They belonged to the Catholic Church, which was the only Christian Church. The head of the Catholic Church was the Pope who lived in Rome.

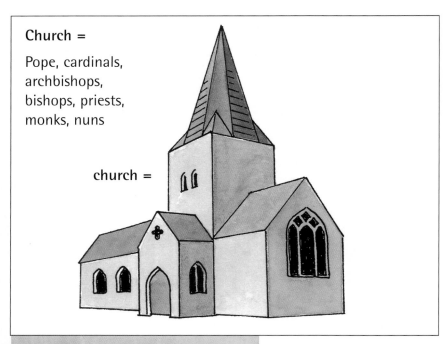

Church =

Pope, cardinals, archbishops, bishops, priests, monks, nuns

church =

The meaning of Church and church.

WHO RAN THE CHURCH?

In England, the Catholic Church was run by two Archbishops – the Archbishop of Canterbury and the Archbishop of York. Under them there were many bishops. When William the Conqueror came to England he owned all the land. He gave out some of it to his barons and also to his bishops.

POWER SHARING IN DURHAM?

In the photograph on page 87 you can see that the castle and the cathedral were close together. In fact, the baron and the bishop were the same person in Durham. He was called the Prince-Bishop and he lived in the castle. In other places, the power was often shared between the local baron and the local bishop. Their large buildings dominated people living in the town close by.

THE WICKED STORY OF WALCHER

Walcher was the first Prince-Bishop at Durham. One day he could be fighting his enemies. The next day he could be taking Mass in the cathedral. Walcher does not seem to have led a very holy life. People suspected him of being involved in the nasty murder of a Saxon man.

The Saxon man's family trapped Walcher in a church at Gateshead. They set fire to the church. Walcher staggered out, half blinded by the smoke and choking. The Saxons were waiting with knives and clubs. They fell on Walcher and killed him.

Not all churchmen were like Walcher. Many were wise and fair.

WHAT WAS CHRISTENDOM

Most people living in Europe in the Middle Ages were Christians. The area of the world where most Christians were living was called Christendom. The map on pages 90 and 91 shows where Christendom was in the Middle Ages.

WAS EVERYONE A CHRISTIAN?

Outside western Europe there were other very important religions. Islam was the religion in the Middle East, parts of southern Europe and northern Africa. There were also Jews in every European country.

SOURCE 2

This map shows you medieval Christendom. The photographs are of medieval churches in different parts of Christendom.

N

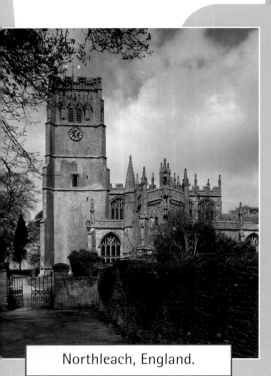

Northleach, England.

Santiago de Compostela, Spain.

Church of the Madeleine, France.

Hagia Sophia, Istanbul.

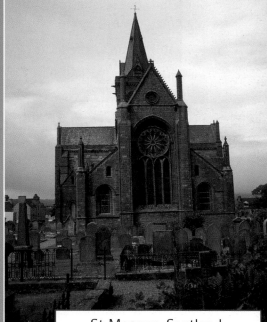
St Magnus, Scotland.

KEY

Christendom

Jerusalem

- What is the same about these churches?
- What is different about these churches?
- Can you suggest reasons for the similarities and the differences?

Question Time

1 Copy the map on pages 90 and 91. Colour in the area of Christendom and put in the key. Mark on the map where each of the churches and cathedrals is.

2 In medieval times churches were built in every village and town. They were looked after by priests. In the cities, much grander churches were built. They were looked after by bishops and they were called cathedrals.

Here is a list of some of the great medieval cathedrals. Use an atlas to find out where these places are and mark them on your map.

- Notre Dame Cathedral in Paris, France.
- Canterbury Cathedral in England.
- Cologne Cathedral in Germany.

3 Go and look at your local parish church. When was it built? If it wasn't built before about 1500 find the medieval church nearest to where you live. Can you start working out why it might have been built where it was?

SOURCE 1

A modern photograph of a village in England.

WHAT IMPACT DID PARISH CHURCHES HAVE ON PEOPLE'S LIVES?

Look at Source 1. What makes the church look important? What is the church built of?

THE CHURCH EVERY DAY

The church in the village reminded people of their duty to God. Every day, they heard the church bells ringing each hour. They saw the big building with its stone tower rising above their own wooden and wattle cottages. They knew the church would be there long after they and their cottages were gone.

THE CHURCH SERVICES

Birth, life and death centred around the church. There were church services every week and special services for special occasions.

- Baptism (parents took their babies to church to be baptised by the priest. This meant that they grew up as Christians).

- Marriage (people married in the church).

- Burials (people were prayed for in the church and buried in the holy ground around it).

- Mass (a church service on Sundays and on holy days).

- Confession (when people told the priest what they had done wrong so that God could forgive them).

WHAT IS MASS?

The Mass is central to Roman Catholic worship. The priest blesses some bread and wine and offers them to God. At that moment, believers think that God changes the bread and wine into the body and blood of Jesus Christ. This is called trans-substantiation.

THE CHURCH AS THE CENTRE OF VILLAGE LIFE

The church was the largest building in the village. The main part of it was used for many things. Sometimes villagers used their church building as a market place. They held feasts, fairs and plays there. Churches also held parties to raise money to keep the church in good repair. A barrel of ale (weak beer) was bought in. Then all the villagers came to buy drinks. The more drinks bought the more money was raised.

Question Time

1 a Look at Source 1. Make a list of the reasons why the church seems to be the most important building in the village.

b Read the following sentence and write whether it is true or false.

Medieval people believed that their Christian religion was very important.

2 a Read the section headed 'The church as the centre of village life'. Make a list of the different activities for which the church building was used. For each activity, say where it would be held today.

b Why have these activities moved out of the church building?

PARISH PRIESTS

The parish was the area
looked after by a priest.
Often it was the same area
as the village. The parish
priest did not marry. His job
was to look after the people
in the parish.

SOURCE 3

A priest treating the sick.

SOURCE 2

A parish priest conducting
a burial.

SOURCE 4

*He truly knew Christ's gospel and would
preach it.*

...he preferred beyond a doubt

Giving to poor parishioners round about

From his own goods and Easter offerings.

*Wide was his parish, with houses far
asunder,*

Yet he neglected not in rain or thunder,

In sickness or in grief, to pay a call

On the remotest, whether great or small.

He did not run to London to earn easy bread

By singing masses for the wealthy dead.

In about 1386, Geoffrey Chaucer wrote a
poem called *The Canterbury Tales*. This is part
of what he wrote about a parish priest.

NOT ALL PRIESTS WERE LIKE THE ONE THAT GEOFFREY CHAUCER DESCRIBED!

SOURCE 5

The ignorance of the priests casteth the people into the ditch of error.

In 1281, Archbishop Peckham wrote this about parish priests.

SOURCE 6

He has been a parish priest for more than 30 years

But he cannot sing the Mass properly, nor read the Bible.

He can't explain the psalms to people.

But he's good at hunting hares in the fields.

In about 1380, William Langland wrote about a parish priest in his poem *Piers Ploughman*.

SOURCE 7

In many parishes, the priest only stumbled through some sermon four times a year

With so feeble a guide, the villager could not get far on his quest for the Truth (in religion).

This is from a book written in 1937 called *Life on the English Manor*.

SOURCE 8

There were many priests who stayed in their parishes and were as good as Chaucer's priest. However, life as a parish priest was too hard to attract men of talent.

From a book written in 1973 called *England in the Later Middle Ages*.

DID THE CHURCH PAY THE PRIESTS?

Priests were not paid money by the church. They had to find other ways to earn money.

Question Time

1 Look at Sources 2–6. Which sources show that priests did good work? Which sources show that some of them did not.

2 Look at Source 4. What sort of good things did Chaucer's priest do?

3 Look at Sources 2–7. How reliable are they as sources of evidence about the life of a parish priest?

HOW THE PRIEST WAS PAID

- Priests collected fees for baptisms, weddings and funerals.

- Priests kept the money collected in the church at Easter.

- Priests could claim the second-best animal from the family when someone in the village died.

- Priests could sell food grown on their land (called the glebe land).

- Priests could keep a small part of the tithe. This was a tax on all the people in the parish. They had to give one-tenth of everything they produced, like grain or wool.

What does it mean?

Tithe
A tax paid to the church.

SOURCE 9

The priest spends his time in taverns ... He is living with a woman and he cannot read or write, and so he cannot look after his parishioners' souls.

This is what one villager said about his priest. He was giving evidence to the Bishop of Hereford in 1397.

SOURCE 10

Ten of the villagers were each fined 2d. They made their sheaves of corn smaller when it was for the tithe. They ought to have made them the same size as they did when working for the Lady of the Manor.

This is what some villagers did to cheat the Church out of tithes. The source is taken from court records.

Question Time

1 How did priests earn money?

2 What different kinds of work did medieval priests do? Make a spidergram with the priest in the middle. Add labels around your priest – choose from the phrases below:

- treat the sick
- deliver televisions
- baptise, marry and bury people
- say Mass
- look after villagers' souls
- programme computers
- read the Bible.

WHAT WOULD CHURCHES BE LIKE INSIDE?

Most Saxon churches were made from wood. New medieval churches were made from stone.

As the Middle Ages continued, some parts of England became rich. People made their churches larger and grander. They put stained glass in the windows, painted pictures on the walls and put gold candlesticks on the altar.

Some of the paintings showed hell and heaven, and encouraged people to be good so they would end up in heaven. These were called 'doom' paintings.

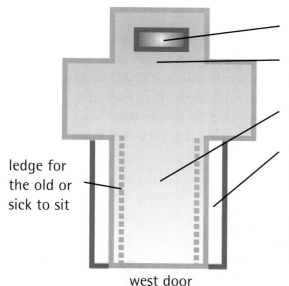

priest celebrated Mass at altar

chancel - only priests and holy people were allowed here

nave - where people stood

aisles were added so processions could be held in church

ledge for the old or sick to sit

west door

Plan of a cross-shaped church.

During the Middle Ages, the Catholic Church became powerful. It became the largest landowner in Christendom. It collected its own taxes and made its own laws. But its real strength was in the power it had over people's minds.

SOURCE 11

Why should I want to go to heaven? I would not wish to go there unless I can have Nicolette, because I love her so much. I want nothing to do with the sort of people who will go to heaven, doddering old priests and fools who grovel in church all day and night.

This is part of a popular medieval story. A young man has been told that if he keeps seeing his girlfriend he will not go to heaven and he might go to hell!

Question Time

❶ Where did the ordinary people stand to listen to the service?

❷ What was the altar for?

❸ Why were aisles added to the church?

HOW COULD THE CATHOLIC CHURCH TELL PEOPLE ABOUT HEAVEN AND HELL?

Most people could not read. The Catholic Church wanted to tell people two things:

- The only way to go to heaven was to obey the teachings of the Catholic Church.

- They would go to hell if they disobeyed.

THE ANSWER

The Church found the answer by using large, terrifying wall paintings (called doom paintings). The paintings would be seen by every man, woman and child each time they went into the church. This would be at least once every Sunday. They would also go in the church at other times during the week. This was because the nave of the church was used as a market and a meeting place.

SOURCE 12

A medieval 'doom' painting showing heaven and hell.

SOURCE 13

To our left was burning flames. On the other side was raging hail and bitter snow blowing in all directions. Both sides were filled with men's souls which seemed to be hurled from one side to the other by the fury of the tempest. Some dark spirits came from the fiery depths and terrified me with their glowing eyes and flames coming from their mouths and nostrils. Then my guide brought me out of darkness into clear light. I saw a lovely meadow. And as my guide led me through the crowds of happy people I wondered whether this was the Kingdom of Heaven.

Taken from *A History of the English Church and People*, written in about 730 AD by the Venerable Bede. It is part of a story told by a man who thought he had returned from the dead.

Life was hard and short for most medieval people. They wondered what it would be like when they died. The Catholic Church gave them the answer: after death there was eternal life in heaven. But eternal life had to be earned.

WHO WENT WHERE?

Heaven

Only people who had followed the teachings of the Catholic Church went straight to heaven.

Purgatory

Most people who were not good enough to go straight to heaven.

Hell

People who had been very wicked and had never asked forgiveness.

'FAST-TRACK' THROUGH PURGATORY?

- Pray for the dead loved ones' souls.
- Light candles for them in holy places.
- Make pilgrimages to holy places.
- Rich people could give money to build special chapels.

What does it mean?

Purgatory
A place where the souls of dead people went, if they had not been good enough to go to heaven. The souls could go from purgatory to heaven.

Pilgrimage
A journey to a special holy place.

Question Time

1 a What two things did the Catholic Church want to tell people in the Middle Ages?

  b Why couldn't they give people a book to read?

2 What is a doom painting?

3 Read Source 13. Make a doom painting of your own.

WHAT IMPACT DID MONKS AND NUNS HAVE ON PEOPLE'S EVERYDAY LIVES?

Medieval monasteries and nunneries tell us something about the ways in which medieval monks and nuns spent their time in the service of God. One problem, however is that most of these buildings in Britain are in ruins.

What does it mean?

Monastery
The group of buildings where monks live and work.

Look at the three pictures carefully.

What clues do the buildings give you about what happened there in medieval times?

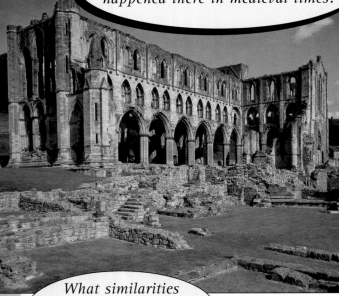

SOURCE 1

Modern photographs of the ruins of Rievaulx (left) and Tintern Abbey (bottom), and an engraving of Citeaux Abbey.

What similarities can you find between the buildings?

What are the building materials?

What shapes are the windows and doorways?

What differences can you find between the buildings?

Question Time

1 Choose one of the buildings on page 100. Find out when it was built and where it was built. Who built it and why did they build it?

2 Compare your findings with what others in your class have found out about that building and the other buildings. Build up an information database. You can add to this later.

CHRISTIANS DEDICATING THEIR LIVES TO GOD

Soon after the death of Jesus Christ, some Christians began to live alone or with a few others. This idea spread. By the Middle Ages there were many small groups of holy people living together. A man called Benedict wrote rules about how such people should live together. Monks and nuns who followed his rules were called Benedictines.

WHAT WAS THE RULE OF ST BENEDICT?

Benedict wrote his rules in about 535AD. They were so sensible that monasteries and other holy houses used his rules. There were rules for everything from praying to farming the monastery's land. Every day a chapter was read to the monks or nuns from St Benedict's rule book. It was read in a special room which became known as the Chapter House. The Chapter House was where all the day's business was discussed.

CHAPTER SIX – CONCERNING SILENCE

This rule told the monks but they must be silent at all times. This was to help them to concentrate on God's work. But for mealtimes (Chapter 38) Benedict said that they could use sign language.

Monks and nuns were not allowed to use too much sign language. It was just as bad for them as talking too much. Gerald of Wales visited Canterbury Cathedral Priory in 1180. He said, 'There were the monks ... all of them signing with fingers, hands and arms, and whistling one to another instead of speaking ... so that I seemed to be seated at a stage play or among the actors and jesters.'

WERE ALL MONKS AND NUNS BENEDICTINES?

In 1066, all monks and nuns in England were Benedictines. Later, other groups followed different rules. These groups were called Cistercians, Carthusians, Augustinians and Gilbertines. Gilbertines existed only in England.

Activity Time

Copy the grid below into your file or exercise book. Research the four Orders, and complete the grid:

	CISTERCIANS	CARTHUSIANS	AUGUSTINIANS	GILBERTINES
When founded?	1098	1084	1104	
Where founded?	Citeaux, in Burgundy, France	French Alps		
Founded by whom?				
Based on whose Rule?		St Benedict	St Augustine	
Why founded?				
Men or women?	Men			Men and women
Known as?	White monks		Black Canons	
Special characteristics?		Each monk slept, ate, worked and prayed in his own room, meeting other monks only occasionally	Monks were all priests who worked outside the monasteries, taking services in parish churches, running schools, hospitals and almshouses	
Buildings in England?	Rievaulx Abbey, North Yorkshire	Mount Grace Priory, North Yorkshire		

WHAT WAS MONASTIC LIFE LIKE?

The first duty of a monk or a nun was prayer. This never changed.

SOURCE 2

A painting of nuns praying in a church.

SOURCE 3

A plan of a monastery called Roche Abbey in about 1350.

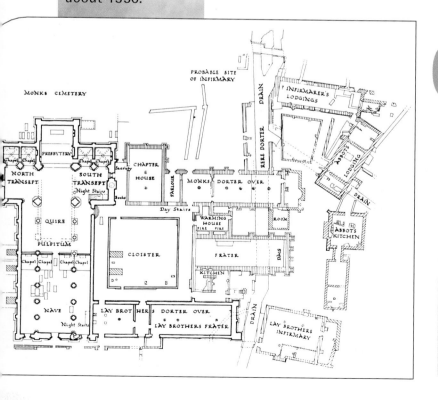

Question Time

1. How does the plan of the monastery show that the monks thought prayer to God was very important?

2. Why were monks and nuns not allowed to do too much signing?

3. How were the monks at Canterbury Cathedral Priory communicating with each other?

4. What did Gerald of Wales think about the monks?

WHAT DID MONKS DO ALL DAY?

Just before the Black Death (1349), monastic life was at its peak. There were about 1000 religious houses containing about 17,000 people. The table below tells you how a choir monk would have spent one of his days in a Cistercian monastery.

Time of day	Activity	Place in abbey
2.00 hrs	VIGILS Church service, done in the dark and from memory	
3.30 hrs	Prayers	Cloister or chapter house
Dawn	LAUDS A short church service	
6.00 hrs (approx)	PRIME Church service and Mass	
7.00 hrs	CHAPTER Holy readings, a chapter from St Benedict's Rule, confess sins and be disciplined. Discuss daily business, given jobs for the day. Start work in the garden, cloisters, workshops, abbey grounds and kitchen etc.	
9.00 hrs	TERCE Church service and holy reading. Work.	
11.30 hrs	SEXT Church service. Wash.	The church and then the laver
12.00 hrs	PRANDIUM Main meal. Bread, two dishes of boiled vegetables, watered wine or weak beer. Rest then wash.	
14.30 hrs	NONES Church service. Drink of water. Work.	
17.30 hrs	VESPERS Church service	
18.00 hrs	Second meal of the day. Bread, fruit and salad.	
18.30 hrs	COLLATION One monk reading aloud.	The church and then the dormitory
20.00 hrs	COMPLINE Church service. Go to bed.	

Question Time

Copy out the table on page 104. Use the plan on page 103 to help you. Fill in the gaps in the third column (place in abbey).

DID MONKS AND NUNS HAVE AN EASY LIFE?

Work through the following sources and make up your own mind!

SOURCE 4

1. All monks must obey the Abbot promptly.

2. All monks shall work in the kitchen.

3. All monks shall work on the farm or in holy reading.

4. A mattress, woollen blanket and pillow is enough for bedding.

5. All the monks are to serve each other, washing the feet of the rest etc.

Some of the rules of St Benedict.

SOURCE 5

These paintings show the sort of work a monk or nun had to do.

SOURCE 6

One of the skeletons found showed signs of arthritis in the knees. The archaeologist in charge of the dig said this was 'hardly surprising for a monk who spends most of his life in a cold church on his knees.'

From *The Times* newspaper, 1987.

WHY DID MEN AND WOMEN BECOME MONKS AND NUNS?

Men became monks and women became nuns for many different reasons.

- They believed they needed to dedicate their lives to God.

- They did not like the life they were living in the ordinary world. Many of them came from large, poor, hungry families.

- They liked the idea of life in a monastery. They could develop new skills.

WHAT DID THE MONASTERY OFFER?

The monastery or nunnery offered a home for life, together with food and clothing, companionship and a sense of purpose. It also offered a chance for men and women to develop particular skills. These skills could be in herbal medicine, teaching, nursing, illustrating manuscripts, music and writing histories.

SOURCE 7

I am tormented by the night prayers. I find the manual labour hard. The rough clothing cuts through my skin. I long for the delights of the world.

Some monks clearly had a hard time!

SOURCE 8

When I was five years old I was put to school.
A priest taught me my letters. Then, oh glorious God, You inspired my father to put me under Your rule. So, weeping, my father sent me away for love of You and never saw me again. And I obeyed him willingly for he promised me in Your name that if I became a monk I should go to heaven after my death.

Oderic Vitalis wrote this when he was 60 years old.

SOURCE 9

Some skilled monks worked as chroniclers (people who wrote about recent history).
Sometimes these monks painted beautiful little pictures in the manuscripts. Much of what we know about medieval times comes from manuscripts some monks have written.

WHAT SORT OF WORK DID MONKS AND NUNS DO?

Monks and nuns did cooking, cleaning, digging and working in the fields. Some of them specialised in running schools and hospitals. Some monasteries were large and had to be well run.

- **The Abbot or Abbess** was in charge of the monastery or nunnery.

- **The Cellarer** ordered supplies and paid bills.

- **The Kitchener** ran the kitchens.

- **The Sacristan** was responsible for valuable things like gold candlesticks.

There were monks and nuns who looked after guests. Some looked after novices (new monks and nuns). Others looked after beggars. But some monasteries were so small that all the monks and nuns shared all the jobs.

SOURCE 10

These pictures show monks at a meeting in the Chapter House and chopping wood.

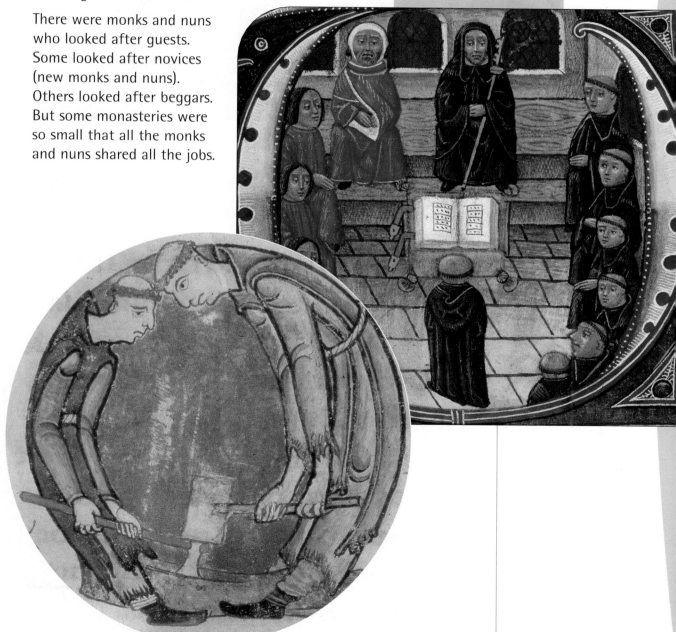

SOURCE 11

Monks and nuns were important in the treatment of the sick. The Church set up hospitals, like St Bartholomew's, in London. The hospitals run by monks and nuns were clean and gave good nursing care.

SOURCE 12

Monks and nuns taught the novices (new monks and nuns) and often ordinary men, women and children from the outside world.

Question Time

1 Look at Source 7. Write down the three things that the monk finds hard.

2 Look at the table on page 104. What would you find the hardest thing about the monk's day?

3 Work with a partner or in a small group. Look at pages 106 to 108. Make a list of all the jobs in a monastery or nunnery. Choose one job and write down the question you would like to ask about it.

WHY DID PEOPLE GO ON PILGRIMAGES?

WHAT IS A PILGRIMAGE?

A pilgrimage is a special journey to a place that people believe is holy. Today, people still go on pilgrimages to holy places. For example, Mecca is the most sacred of all the Muslim cities. Muhammad, who started the Muslim religion, was born there. Each year, about 2 million Muslims make a pilgrimage to Mecca. In medieval times, people also went on pilgrimages to their holy places.

WHO WENT ON PILGRIMAGES?

All sorts of people went on pilgrimages in medieval times. Kings went on pilgrimages. So did butchers, bakers, priests and housewives.

WHY DID PEOPLE GO ON PILGRIMAGES?

People went on pilgrimages for many different reasons.

- To cure themselves of an illness.

- To ask for a special favour.

- To give thanks because something wonderful had happened.

- To speed their way, or a loved one's way, through purgatory.

- To have a holiday.

WHERE DID MEDIEVAL CHRISTIANS GO ON PILGRIMAGE?

The most holy place was Jerusalem in the Holy Land, where Jesus Christ had lived. The second most holy place was Rome, where the Pope lived. But most people could not travel so far.

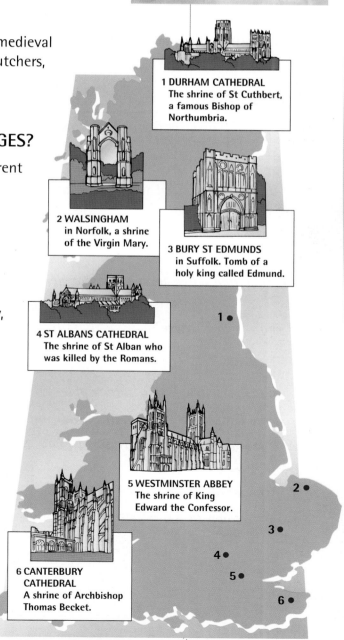

This map shows where the main shrines were in England.

1 DURHAM CATHEDRAL
The shrine of St Cuthbert, a famous Bishop of Northumbria.

2 WALSINGHAM
in Norfolk, a shrine of the Virgin Mary.

3 BURY ST EDMUNDS
in Suffolk. Tomb of a holy king called Edmund.

4 ST ALBANS CATHEDRAL
The shrine of St Alban who was killed by the Romans.

5 WESTMINSTER ABBEY
The shrine of King Edward the Confessor.

6 CANTERBURY CATHEDRAL
A shrine of Archbishop Thomas Becket.

HOW DID PILGRIMS TRAVEL?

Most people travelled to a shrine or a holy place in their own country. Pilgrims usually travelled in groups. This was partly for safety. Most people walked. Only the very rich could travel on horseback. Along famous pilgrim routes there were inns and hostels where pilgrims could stay. But many poor pilgrims slept in the hedgerows.

WHAT MADE A PLACE HOLY?

Most holy places were shrines. They were often in a church or a cathedral. Shrines were places where relics were kept. A relic might be something like a saint's finger bone. Some relics were a bit dubious: for instance the feather from an angel's wing. However the important thing was that people believed the relics were holy.

What does it mean?

Relic
An object that has special religious meaning.

SOURCE 1

This is what Chaucer wrote about some pilgrims:

The cook
Many a pilgrim's cursed you more than sparsely

When suffering the effects of your stale parsley

Which they had eaten with your stubble-fed goose;

Your shop is one where many a fly is loose.

The miller
The miller, very drunk and rather pale

Was straddled on his horse half on half off

'First I'm bound to say I'm drunk. I know it by my sound.

And if the words get muddled in my tale

Just put it down to too much Southwark ale.'

The franklin
He lived for pleasure and had always done ...

His house was never short of bake-meat pies,

Or fish and flesh and these in such supplies

It positively snowed with meat and drink

And all the dainties that a man could think.

The doctor
The cause of every malady you'd got

He knew, and whether dry, cold, moist or hot

All his apothecaries in a tribe

Were redeemed with the drugs he would prescribe ...

Gold stimulates the heart, or so we're told.

He therefore had a special love of gold.

GEOFFREY CHAUCER AND THE CANTERBURY TALES

We know some things about Geoffrey Chaucer's life. He was born around 1343. He was the son of a wealthy wine merchant. When Geoffrey Chaucer was a boy, he worked as a page in the household of King Richard II. When he was about 16 years old he was fighting in the Hundred Years' War.

After that Chaucer went on trade and diplomatic missions to Italy and France. He was a customs controller in London and a Clerk of Works at Westminster. We know that he married Philippa Roet, who worked at the royal court. They had two sons.

The ploughman

For steadily about his work he went

To thrash his corn, to dig or to manure

Or make a ditch; and he would help the poor

For love of Christ and never take a penny

If he could help it, and, as prompt as any,

He paid his tithes in full when they were due.

A wife from Bath

A worthy woman all her life, what's more

She'd had five husbands, all at the Church door.

And she had thrice been to Jerusalem,

Seen many strange rivers and passed over them;

She'd been to Rome ...

She knew the remedies for love's mischances,

An art in which she knew the oldest dances.

WHY IS GEOFFREY CHAUCER IMPORTANT?

Geoffrey Chaucer did many jobs. But he is remembered for being a poet. His best-known poem is called *The Canterbury Tales*. It is about 12 people who are making a pilgrimage to the tomb of St Thomas Becket in Canterbury Cathedral.

Question Time

❶ Use a copy of a map of Britain. Look at the map on page 109. Label your map with each of the holy places.

❷ You are a poor person and you want to go on a pilgrimage to a holy place. How will you travel?

❸ You are living in a tiny village near Birmingham. Which holy place will you choose to go to? Use an atlas to help you.

❹ You are a fairly good walker so you can walk about three to four miles every hour. Work out how long it will take you on your pilgrimage.

❺ Explain why you are going on your pilgrimage (see page 109).

❻ What can we learn from Chaucer about life in medieval England?

WAS EVERYONE IN ENGLAND A CHRISTIAN?

Everyone in Britain was expected to be a Christian. There was one exception to this: the Jews.

WHEN DID THE JEWS COME TO ENGLAND?

Most Jews came to England after 1066. The Jews had helped William the Conqueror raise money for his invasion of England. They carried on being useful to William and all the Norman kings after him. This was because they lent the king money.

WHY DIDN'T CHRISTIANS LEND THE KING MONEY?

The Christian Church forbade money-lending. Money-lending was called usury. The Jews were not Christians so they were not bound by the same rules.

WHERE DID THE JEWS LIVE?

At first Jews settled in London. They were under the protection of the king. As the years went by Jews were living in other cities like Norwich, Oxford, Cambridge, Winchester, Exeter, York and Canterbury. They lived separately from Christians. They usually lived in a particular area close to the synagogue. This was the place where they went to worship.

DID THE JEWS DO ANYTHING ELSE APART FROM LEND MONEY?

It was difficult for Jews living in England to work with Christians. In the Middle Ages people agreed a contract by swearing a Christian oath. Jews could not swear a Christian oath. This meant they could not agree to buy or sell land or do any other business with Christians. Therefore, most Jews made most of their money as money-lenders.

TO WHOM DID THE JEWS LEND MONEY?

- Kings.
- The Catholic Church (Jews helped to fund the Crusades and the building of Fountains Abbey).
- Merchants and country gentleman.
- Anyone who needed to borrow money (people who were punished by a fine in the courts often went to Jewish money-lenders for a loan).

WHY DID PEOPLE START PERSECUTING THE JEWS?

It was in the king's interest to protect the Jews. Kings borrowed enormous sums of money from the Jews. They also taxed the Jews heavily. As the years went by, many people were borrowing from Jewish money-lenders. They resented the high level of interest they had to pay to the Jews. They wanted to find ways to get out of making debt repayments. So the monarch, the Church and the people gradually turned on the Jews.

TROUBLE IN NORWICH AND OTHER CITIES

Christian people began to unfairly blame Jews when things went wrong. In 1144, an apprentice disappeared. He was found murdered in a wood near Norwich. Rumours spread that he had been killed by Jews. There was absolutely no evidence that any Jew had been involved in his death. Trouble also started in London and then spread to other cities. Christians began taunting Jews. In some towns, Jewish houses and shops were attacked and burnt.

TROUBLE IN YORK

In 1190, some Jewish families fled to York Castle, chased by a mob. The leader of the mob owed local Jews a lot of money. The mob surrounded the castle and demanded that the Jews became Christians. In desperation, fathers cut the throats of their wives and children and then gave themselves up. They were then killed by the mob. The rioting ended with the townspeople making a giant bonfire of the records of loans made to them by Jews.

SOURCE 1

In their churches (synagogues) Jews must worship quietly. Jews must not have Christian servants. Jews must not eat with Christians. Jews must not have Christians in their house. Jews must wear a badge. Jews must have a special licence to go and live in a town.

From a law made by Henry III in 1253.

THINGS GET WORSE

In some places Jews and Christians got along well together. However, more and more laws were passed that made life difficult for Jews:

- They had to wear a special badge to show they were Jews.

- They were taxed more and more heavily.

- They were not allowed to leave precious belongings in their parish church for safe-keeping.

To many people, it seemed that the Christian Church was agreeing with the bad treatment of Jews. This made things worse for Jews.

THE JEWS LEAVE ENGLAND

Edward I passed a law in 1290 that expelled the Jews from England. There were about 3000 Jews living in England then. They sold up what remained of their possessions and left. They did not come back for nearly 400 years.

SOURCE 2

These enemies of Christ have made Christian folk poor by their usuries. They have forced many Christians to sell their lands and goods. These people should depart forever.

From a law against the Jews passed by Edward I in 1290.

Question Time

1 Why did a lot of Jews come to England after 1066?

2 Why didn't Christians lend money?

3 Why did people start persecuting the Jews?

4 Do you think living separately helped or hindered the Jews and Christians getting on together?

RUMBLINGS OF DISCONTENT?

Not everyone was happy with the Catholic Church.

CRITICISMS OF MONKS, NUNS AND FRIARS

SOURCE 1

The Cistercian monks work hard so they become rich. But they do not help other people by lending farm equipment. When they are given new lands they throw the people out of the villages there.

Walter Map wrote this in the twelfth century.

SOURCE 3

The friars have no time for the poor. No one can be buried in one of their graveyards unless he leaves them some money in his will.

From *Piers Ploughman* by William Langland, written in about 1380.

SOURCE 2

When Samson became abbot he gave a dinner for a 1000 guests. He had several parks made for the abbey. He stocked them with wild animals and kept a huntsman and hounds.

Jocelin of Brakelond wrote this about the Benedictine monastery of Bury St. Edmunds in the thirteenth century.

SOURCE 4

William Swinderby was a priest in Leicester. He said that people should not pay tithes to lazy priests. The bishop was angry with him and banned him from churches. So he preached in the street and crowds flocked to hear him.

A monk in Leicester, called Henry Knighton, wrote this in 1390.

SOURCE 5

A medieval manuscript showing nuns going back to their abbey after a night of fun.

JOHN WYCLIFFE AND THE LOLLARDS

John Wycliffe lectured at Oxford University between 1372 and 1382. He was protected by a great nobleman called John of Gaunt. This meant that Wycliffe could say what he thought.

WYCLIFFE CRITICISED THE CHURCH

Wycliffe said:

- Priests were often wealthy and ignorant.

- A person's belief should be based on the Bible alone and not on what priests told him or her.

- The Bible should be translated from Latin into English so more people could read it.

- The bread and wine used in the Mass might not change into flesh and blood.

- There was no need for a Pope because Christ was head of the Church.

WYCLIFFE'S IDEAS SPREAD

Wycliffe and his followers preached in towns and villages all over England. Wycliffe's followers were called Lollards. This was a nickname because people said they mumbled.

What the Church did

The Church arrested and tried the Lollards in church courts. Some Lollards were burned at the stake for their ideas.

Could the Church stop the rot?

The Church put down the Lollards but it could not stop:

- people thinking for themselves
- people wanting to take the riches of the monasteries
- kings wanting to stop sharing power in England with the Church.

MEDIEVAL PEOPLE

Question Time

1 a Which five different types of Church people are Sources 1–5 about?

b How reliable are Sources 1–5 as evidence of people's unhappiness with the Catholic Church?

2 Who were the Lollards?

MAUD
the BREWER

Lives in a small village
Widowed with three children
Finds it hard to pay tithes
A grumbler

GARTH
the PIG-MAN

Works for a harsh lord of the manor
Unmarried
Goes to church frequently
Always looks on the bright side

**JOHN
the SILVERSMITH**

Lives in a large town
Married with four children
Has been on a pilgrimage
A worrier

**CLARA
the BUSINESSWOMAN**

Widowed twice – Rich
Trades in woollen cloth
Gives to churches and monasteries
A careful planner

**DOMINIC
the FRIAR**

Preaches in markets and fairs
Unmarried
Does not want any possessions
Quietly hopeful

WILFRED the MONK

Works as a cellarer
Helped make his monastery rich
Ambitious

Activity Time

How did the medieval Church affect people's lives?

Choose one of the characters above. How would the person you have chosen answer the question: 'How has the Church affected your life?'

Unit 5: Elizabeth 1 – how successfully did she tackle the problems of her reign?

WHY WAS RELIGION A LIFE OR DEATH PROBLEM IN ELIZABETHAN ENGLAND?

SOURCE 1

Campion and another Jesuit visit England in 1580. What is his future? Look in the background for clues.

An artist's reconstruction of John Stubbs having his hand cut off.

EDMUND CAMPION

Campion was a Jesuit priest. He came to England to convert people back to being Catholic. Elizabeth's government spies caught him hiding in a house where he was saying Mass. He was put on trial. He said that he was just a religious man. The government said that he was a traitor to the queen.

Campion was executed in 1581. More than 100 other Jesuit priests were executed for the same reason. Religion was very close to politics in Elizabethan England.

JOHN STUBBS

The drawing at the bottom of page 120 shows John Stubbs being punished by having his right hand chopped off.

Why was he being punished?

Stubbs had printed a book that criticised Elizabeth for thinking of marrying a Catholic. Stubbs was a very strict Protestant. Very strict Protestants were called Puritans. Elizabeth wanted everyone to belong to the Church of England. She felt threatened by both Catholics and Puritans.

What did Stubbs say?

Which of the lines below do you think Stubbs was heard to say as soon as his punishment had been performed?

a) Long live Protestantism!

b) Long live the Puritans!

c) God save the queen!

The answer is c. Perhaps he wanted to impress Elizabeth.

RELIGION IN ELIZABETHAN ENGLAND

Problems over religion had existed since Henry VIII broke away from the Pope and the Catholic Church. Under Elizabeth, the Church of England was the official religion of the country. Everyone was expected to be of the same religion as the monarch. To go against this was to be a traitor. It could be very dangerous. If you did not go to church you could be fined.

Question Time

❶ What was Campion doing when he was caught by Elizabeth's government spies?

❷ According to the government, what crime had he committed?

❸ What did he say he was?

❹ Campion was loyal to Queen Elizabeth and had not stolen anything or murdered anyone. Why was Campion executed?

❺ What does the story of Stubbs tell you about the importance of

a religion

b the power of the monarch in this period?

WHY WAS RELIGION SO IMPORTANT IN THE SIXTEENTH CENTURY?

Religion affected everyone. People believed that God was responsible for everything that happened on Earth and where everyone would go after death.

WHY DID THE CONCEPTION OF ELIZABETH PRESENT A PROBLEM TO HER FATHER?

HENRY VIII – HIS WIFE AND HIS MISTRESS

Elizabeth's mother, Anne Boleyn, was Henry's mistress. She became pregnant in 1532. Henry was delighted but he had a problem. He was married to Catherine of Aragon. She was 48 years old and they had a daughter, Mary. Henry desperately wanted a son to succeed him as king. He thought that Anne's child might be a boy, so he wanted to divorce Catherine and marry Anne. Then his children by Anne would be his legitimate heirs. The problem was how to divorce Catherine.

WAS HENRY REALLY MARRIED TO CATHERINE?

Henry wondered if he was really married to Catherine. She had been married to his brother, Arthur, who died. Maybe the fact that Henry and Catherine had no son was God's way of punishing Henry for marrying his brother's widow.

DIVORCE AND THE POPE

Only the Pope could give a divorce. The Pope refused. Catherine was the aunt of the Emperor Charles V who had a strong influence on the Pope. Henry began to wonder whether he could set up his own Church in England. Then he could give his own divorce.

SOURCE 1

If the Pope is unwilling (to give a divorce), we are left to find a cure elsewhere.

From a letter to the Pope signed by English lords and bishops in 1530.

What does it mean?

Conception
The beginning of a person's life when their mother becomes pregnant.

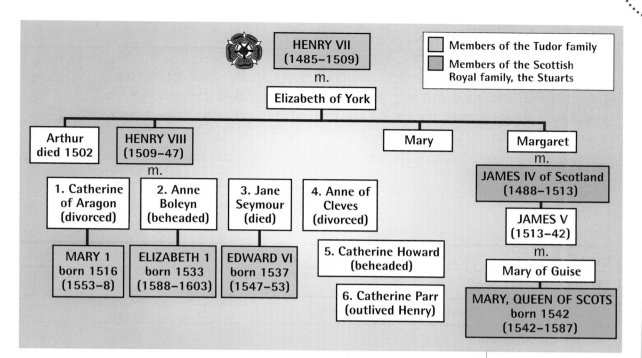

OUT WITH THE POPE?

What did the Pope and being Catholic mean in England at this time?

- The Pope was head of the Catholic Church.

- The Pope was in control of the entire Catholic Church. People paid taxes to the Pope.

- The Pope was the only person who could give divorces to Christians.

- Nearly everyone in England was Catholic. Catholic traditions were popular.

- If England stopped being Catholic, other Catholic countries might look on England as an enemy.

- The monasteries in England were rich, powerful and Catholic. They owned a lot of land. Henry might have to act against them if he split with the Pope.

Henry wanted to move away from being under the control of the Pope and the Catholic Church. But what would this mean for him and for England?

Question Time

1 Read Source 1. What do you think that this letter means when it mentions a 'cure'?

2 What is the general message to the Pope from the English lords and bishops? Choose from the list below.

a The lords and bishops will support Henry against the Pope.

b The lords and bishops will not support Henry against the Pope.

Question Time

The word 'consequences' means the results of an action. Read the section on page 123 that is headed 'Out with the Pope?' Work out what the consequences might be if Henry ignored the Pope. Copy and fill in the chart with your ideas.

If Henry ignored the Pope and the Catholic Church what might happen to:	Benefits for Henry	Problems for Henry
The Pope?		
English people's lives?		
Catholic countries abroad?		
Henry's unborn child?		
Henry's power?		
Money in England?		
Land in England?		

1 Are there more benefits or problems on your consequences chart?

2 Circle or colour in the two most important consequences on your chart. Compare your choices with the rest of the class.

3 Henry had to weigh up the consequences of ignoring the Pope. What action would he take?

a Stay Catholic and stay with Catherine of Aragon and hope she might have a boy.

b Stay Catholic and hope that Anne Boleyn, his mistress, has a boy.

c Break away from the Catholic Church and the Pope, divorce Catherine and marry Anne.

What are the advantages of each of these alternatives? What are the disadvantages?

HENRY'S DECISION

Henry decided to ignore the Pope.

- He set up his own Church. He called himself 'Head of the Church of England.'

- He gave himself a divorce from Catherine and married Anne.

These actions changed the history of England. Was it all to do with Anne?

WHAT CAUSED THE ENGLISH REFORMATION?

The changing of the official religion in England is called the English Reformation. There were a number of causes of the Reformation.

The state of the Church

The Catholic Church had been criticised for years. People said it was too rich and powerful. Monks had moved away from worshipping God and living simple lives. They were accused of drinking, gambling and having wives. Two of the critics were:

* John Wycliffe (1320–84)
* Martin Luther (1483–1546).

Protestantism

In Germany, Martin Luther protested that people did not need the Catholic Church. They should just believe in God and Jesus and learn about Christianity from the Bible. This started Protestantism, from the word 'protest'. These new Protestant ideas spread across Europe. Germany, Switzerland and the Netherlands all became Protestant by the 1540s.

What does it mean?

Reformation
When the religion in England was changed from Catholic to Protestant.

Money

Henry wanted to be a powerful king. He went to war against France and Scotland. This cost a great deal of money. Henry's luxurious lifestyle also cost money. He needed to raise as much money as possible.

Henry's advisers

Thomas Cromwell was Henry's main adviser. He and the Archbishop of Canterbury, Thomas Cranmer, advised Henry about politics and religion. They told Henry that he could be head of his own church and grant his own divorce.

An heir to the throne?

In 1532 Anne Boleyn became pregnant. This meant that if Henry could marry her and have a son, he would have a male heir to the throne. He needed to divorce Catherine quickly. He also wanted everyone to believe that he had never really been married to Catherine. Anne was his proper wife and so their son would be the next king.

Question Time

What caused the Reformation?

1 Look at pages 125 and 126. Match the boxes below to make three of the causes of the Reformation.

The new ideas in religion

meant that many people did not trust Catholicism as much

Problems with the Catholic Church

so he had control of everything from divorce to church lands

Henry was advised to set up his own church

meant that some people were keen to introduce Protestantism

2 Below is a list of causes of the Reformation. Some are long-term causes (things that had been going on for a long time). Some are short-term causes (the trigger that made the Reformation happen in England). Decide which are long-term and which are short-term causes.

- Monasteries had been criticised for many years for being too rich. Many monks and nuns lived idle lives.

- The Catholic Church was very powerful. For many years monarchs had resented its power in England.

- Henry VIII wanted to divorce Catherine and marry Anne. The Pope would not let him do it.

- In Germany, Martin Luther protested that people did not need the Catholic Church. This suddenly brought to a head all the criticism of the Catholic Church. It happened around the same time that Henry wanted a divorce.

- Henry needed money to fight wars and live luxuriously. If he controlled the Church in England, he could control the Church's money.

THE LAST LAUGH

After all Henry went through to set up a new Church, divorce Catherine and marry Anne to produce a male heir, Anne had a baby girl.

WHAT RELIGIOUS CHANGES WERE TAKING PLACE IN THE REST OF EUROPE?

COMPLAINTS ABOUT THE CHURCH

In the 1300s, John Wycliffe said the Church was too rich and powerful.

In 1516, a man called Erasmus said that everyone (not just priests) should be able to read the Bible. This meant translating it from Latin into other languages.

Martin Luther nailed his 95 complaints to the church door at Wittenberg.

MARTIN LUTHER COMPLAINS

Martin Luther was a Catholic priest in Germany. In 1517 he wrote out a list of 95 things that were wrong with the Catholic Church. He nailed the list to the church door in Wittenberg. He wanted everyone to read what he thought.

LUTHER'S TOP SIX COMPLAINTS

1 People should not have to speak to God through a priest.

2 Faith in God is the most important thing for getting to heaven.

3 Going on pilgrimages and to Mass is less important than believing in Jesus Christ.

4 People cannot read the Bible for themselves because it is written in Latin.

5 The Pope should not be overall ruler in every country.

6 Only God forgives people's sins. Indulgence (buying a pardon for a sin from a priest) is wrong.

Many people were interested in Luther's ideas.

Luther also criticised the wealth and power of the Catholic Church.
He was ordered to explain himself to the Emperor.

Question Time

1 Read Luther's top six complaints.

a What is the most important thing for getting to heaven?

b What is less important than believing in Jesus Christ?

c Why couldn't people read the Bible for themselves?

d Who forgives people's sins?

e What was an indulgence?

2 Which suggestion do you think would be the most unpopular with:

a the Pope

b Catholic priests

c ordinary Catholics?

Luther was excommunicated (expelled) from the Catholic Church. He burnt the excommunication letter from the Pope.

PROTESTANTISM SPREADS ACROSS EUROPE

Luther's complaints made many people realise that they too were unhappy with the Catholic Church. In this way Luther, and another preacher called John Calvin, introduced Protestantism into Europe.

Luther's ideas spread across Europe, helped by the invention of the new printing presses.

DIFFERENT TYPES OF PROTESTANTISM

People took on the ideas of Luther and Calvin in different ways so there were different types of Protestantism in different countries.

What does it mean?

Excommunication
This means cutting someone off from membership of the Church.

Luther's new ideas about religion formed the start of Protestantism.

PROTESTANTISM WAS POPULAR WITH KINGS

Many kings and leaders liked Protestantism. There were three main reasons for this:

- They would be independent from the Pope and the Church.

- They could claim all the taxes that usually went to the Church.

- Many of them believed the Church needed to reform (change for the better).

THE COUNTER-REFORMATION

The Catholic Church was afraid of Protestantism. It started its own Counter-Reformation. Protestants were put on trial for heresy (believing in ideas against a religion). Some people were fined and excommunicated. Other people were imprisoned or burned to death.

Question Time

Look at the map below. Would you say that the spread of Protestantism was more successful in northern Europe than in southern Europe?

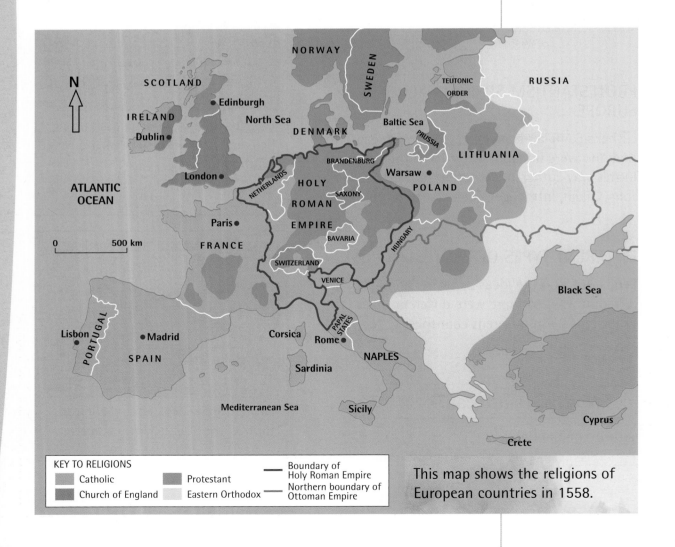

This map shows the religions of European countries in 1558.

WHAT DID ELIZABETH DO ABOUT THE RELIGIOUS PROBLEM IN ENGLAND?

Henry VIII introduced the Reformation in England. He made himself Head of the Church, divorced Catherine and married Anne. Then he stopped. He did not make changes to the way in which people worshipped in the churches.

When Henry died, his son Edward became king. Edward was a strict Protestant. He changed the way in which people worshipped in churches.

When Edward died his sister Mary became queen. She was Catherine's daughter and she was a strict Catholic. She changed everything back to the old Catholic ways of worshipping. She had Protestants burned at the stake.

SOURCE 1

Holy bread and holy water were given, altars were redecorated, pictures were put up and the cross and a crucifix were carried in processions. English services stopped in churches. Latin services started again.

From a book about the changes Mary made as queen.

SOURCE 2

All images were pulled down in churches in England. All the walls of the churches were painted with whitewash. The Commandments were written on the walls.

From writings about the changes Edward made when he became king.

THE CHANGES IN THE CHURCH AND ITS SERVICES

	Catholic churches and church services	Protestant churches and church services	Churches and services under Elizabeth I
Decoration of building	• wall-paintings		
Layout of building			
Priests/ministers		• wear plain robes	
Language used		• English Prayer Book	
Style of services			

Interior of a Protestant church in Edward's reign.

plain glass in window

plain cross

Bible (in English)

plain table

white-washed walls

priest with simple robes

Interior of a Catholic church in Mary's reign.

rood screen

crucifix

ornate altar cloth

paintings on walls

altar boy with incense

priest with ornate robes

stained glass window

ELIZABETH'S RELIGIOUS CHANGES

Mary died in 1558 and Elizabeth became queen. People were tired of all the religious changes. Elizabeth was determined to keep the country at peace. She was a Protestant, but she knew that Edward's strict Protestantism was very unpopular with Catholics. She knew that Mary's strict Catholicism was unpopular with Protestants. Elizabeth wanted a middle way. She got Parliament to pass a Religious Settlement to make Protestant religion law. She was the governor of the Church of England.

Question Time

❶ Look at Sources 1 and 2 and the drawings on this page. Copy out the chart on page 131. Complete the first two columns of the chart to show what Catholic and Protestant churches were like in this period.

❷ Now read Source 3 on page 133. Complete the third column in the chart on page 131.

Factfile:
Elizabeth's Religious Settlement

Parliament passed laws saying that:

- Elizabeth was the rightful monarch.
- Elizabeth was in charge of the Church.
- Everyone must use the same English Prayer Book.
- Every church must use an English Bible.
- Priests must wear the old style vestments (robes).

Some Protestants thought the new Church of England was too like the Catholic Church. On the whole, most people followed Elizabeth's religious settlement.

SOURCE 3

At first even Catholics did not see any great change from the Catholic religion in the new religion set up by Queen Elizabeth, apart from the different language (changed to English).

Written by a lawyer who later became a Catholic monk.

ELIZABETH'S RELIGIOUS ENEMIES

Most people accepted Elizabeth's Religious Settlement. However there were two groups who disliked it. These groups were:

- the Jesuits
- the Puritans.

I am a Jesuit priest.

The Jesuit Society was set up in 1543.

We protect the Catholic religion against heretics (people who go against the Catholic faith).

We want old-style services and the Mass in Latin.

Bishops and priests are important as they guide people to God.

The Pope is God's leader of the Church on Earth.

I am a Puritan.

We are against the old corrupt Catholic Church.

Our leaders are chosen by ourselves; we are all equal.

People can talk to God on their own and through reading the Bible.

Latin Mass, music, decorated vestments (robes worn by priests) just take people's minds away from God.

Question Time

1 What do the Jesuits want?

2 How are the Puritan leaders chosen?

3 Why did the Puritans dislike Elizabeth's Religious Settlement?

WERE CATHOLICS OR PURITANS THE GREATER THREAT TO ELIZABETH'S RELIGIOUS SETTLEMENT?

Read all about it!

Fines increased for not going to church

Campion hung, drawn and quartered for treason

Stubbs hand cut off

The queen excommunicated by the Pope!

These headlines are describing events in Elizabeth's reign. Was Campion a Catholic or a Puritan? Was Stubbs a Catholic or a Puritan? Look back at pages 120 and 121 to remind you.

HOW SERIOUS A THREAT WERE THE CATHOLICS?

In 1570 Elizabeth was excommunicated by the Pope. This meant that she was expelled from the Catholic Church. The Pope told the English Catholics that they did not have to obey Elizabeth any more.

What does it mean?

Treason
Doing something that can seriously harm your monarch and your country.

SECRET CATHOLICS AND DETERMINED CATHOLICS

Most Catholics were happy to accept Elizabeth as their monarch. They just carried on being Catholics in secret. But some English Catholics agreed with the Pope. They were determined that England must be Catholic again.

PRIESTS AND PRIEST HOLES

The Pope sent Jesuit (Catholic) priests to England. They were smuggled into the country and hidden by rich Catholic families. Often secret rooms were built in houses. They were called priest holes. The priests held secret Masses for the rich Catholics and their friends.

The Catholics had to be careful. In the 1580s Elizabeth became very worried about the Catholic threat to her country because:

- relations with Catholic Spain were bad
- Elizabeth had already discovered Catholic plots against her
- Elizabeth knew that many English Catholics had contacts with Catholics in Spain and France.

ELIZABETH TAKES ACTION

Elizabeth's Parliament passed laws against the Catholics. Fines were increased for not going to church. This forced many poorer Catholics back to the Church of England. However, Elizabeth knew that fines did not matter to rich Catholics.

Elizabeth sent soldiers to search Catholic houses to find the hidden Catholic priests. If they were found they could be executed for treason.

Elizabeth's clever minister, Walsingham set up a spy network. He managed to track down over 100 Catholic priests.

SOURCE 1

Elizabeth, the pretended Queen of England ... has helped many heretics. This very woman has taken the country and ruined it ... She should be cut off from the Church and deprived of all her power. Her subjects (people) are freed from obeying her on any matter.

From the Papal Bull of 1570.

SOURCE 2

Catholic priests about to be hanged. They would then be drawn (dragged through the streets on a hurdle) and quartered (cut into four pieces) while still alive.

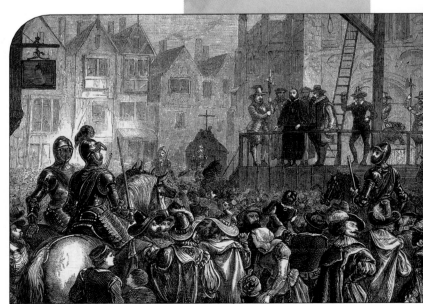

SOURCE 3

There are many people who differ in some opinions of religion from the Church of England, but they do stay loyal and obedient to her Majesty. None of these are charged with any crimes of treason.

One of Elizabeth's ministers explaining that many Catholics are not a threat.

HOW SERIOUS A THREAT WERE THE PURITANS?

The Puritans thought that Elizabeth's Church of England was too Catholic. A large number of MPs were Puritan. They argued loudly in Parliament for changes. They wanted a new Prayer Book. They wanted the Church of England to be more Protestant.

WHAT DID ELIZABETH DO?

Elizabeth ignored the Puritans as much as she could. She did not want to upset the Catholics. The Puritan threat faded away but it returned in the next century.

Question Time

❶ Look at the headlines on page 135. What do they tell us about religion under Elizabeth's rule? Read the sentences below and write true or false about each of them.

- Nobody cared about religion.
- People were prepared to die for their religion.
- Elizabeth's rule was threatened by the power of the Pope.
- Religion was a very important part of life.
- Most people did not go to church.

❷ What could the message in Source 1 mean for Catholics in England?

❸ Look at Source 2. Why would Catholics want to draw pictures of these priests being hanged, drawn and quartered? Why would Protestants want to draw pictures of the same thing?

SOURCE 4

Their feast days, may-games, sports, plays and shows led people away from the fear of God. The days set forth for holy days were usually the times when they most dishonoured God by those things.

George Fox, a Puritan, complaining about activities on holy days such as Sundays.

SOURCE 5

At the beginning they argued over just a hat or a gown that priests wear. Now it has grown to bishops and archbishops ... These men want all religious ministers to be equal. They would also want to deprive the queen of her authority and give it to the people.

A warning about the challenge of Puritans to Elizabeth's power.

SOURCE 6

All priests must accept:
- *Elizabeth's authority as queen*
- *that they will use only the Book of Common Prayer in services*
- *the basic ideas about religion set down in the Religious Settlement.*

All priests had to accept these basic ideas or they could be thrown out of the Church.

Question Time

Elizabeth dealt harshly with the Puritans as well as the Catholics.

Who do you think posed the greater threat to Elizabeth? Hold a debate or a class discussion to find an answer. You should discuss the points below.

- foreign contacts
- obedience to the queen
- criticisms of the queen's ideas.

Activity Time

You are a Puritan. Design a poster to show what Puritans want. Be careful not to criticise Queen Elizabeth. It could be dangerous.

WHY DID MARY, QUEEN OF SCOTS, POSE SUCH A BIG PROBLEM FOR THE QUEEN?

By 1563 Elizabeth had introduced her Religious Settlement. She had solved the main religious problems, but her reign was not free from trouble. In the 1580s a series of plots against Elizabeth was discovered.

SOURCE 1

A painting of the execution of Mary, Queen of Scots, 1587.

Den VIII february werde onthalst Maria
Stuart Schots Coninginne, tekenende Roomsch Catho-

DEATH OF A PRISONER, 1587

After months of indecision, Elizabeth agreed to sign an important piece of paper. It was a death warrant to execute a prisoner. Elizabeth convinced herself that she had no choice. The law had found the prisoner guilty. The messenger quickly took the news to Fotheringay Castle where the prisoner was held.

The prisoner was to have her head cut off. She was praying aloud in Latin as she knelt down. A woman gave her some dignity by placing a cloth over her face. It took two blows of the axe to remove her head.

Factfile: Mary, Queen of Scots

Mary in France

- Mary became Queen of Scotland as a baby, She was brought up as a Catholic in her mother's home in France.
- Mary married Francis who became King of France. She hardly spoke any Scottish or English.
- Francis died in 1560 and Mary returned to Scotland as queen.

Mary in Scotland

- Mary was Catholic. Scotland was Protestant.
- Mary married the Catholic Lord Darnley. Darnley had Mary's secretary Rizzio murdered.
- Darnley's house was blown up and he was strangled.
- Mary's new 'friend' James, Earl of Bothwell was suspected of the murder. Soon after, Mary married Bothwell. The Scottish nobles felt that Mary was not only Catholic, but she was not to be trusted.
- Mary was chased out of Scotland. Her baby son, James, became King James VI of Scotland.

Mary in England

- Mary went to her cousin Elizabeth for help.
- Elizabeth was in a difficult situation. Mary was her cousin and she was a fellow queen. But Mary had always made it clear that she thought she had the true claim to the English throne.
- Elizabeth had Mary imprisoned in various country houses in England.
- Parliament kept trying to persuade Elizabeth to have Mary executed for treason because she was the focus for any Catholic group who wanted to get rid of Elizabeth.

After the second fall of the axe the executioner held up the head for everyone to see. The crowd was shocked to see the grey hair of the prisoner as her wig fell to the ground.

News of the execution reached Elizabeth. She screamed, shouted and demanded answers. She had not meant this to happen. The prisoner was her cousin, Mary, Queen of Scots. She would live with this guilt for the rest of her life.

THE PROBLEM: WHAT TO DO WITH MARY, QUEEN OF SCOTS.

Before her death, Mary had been a focus for Catholic plotters.

- She could ally (take sides) with Catholic countries like Spain and France.

- England's relations with Spain were already bad at this time.

- There had been several Catholic plots against Elizabeth. Had Mary been involved in them?

Question Time

1 Look at the Factfile on page 140.

   a What religion was Mary, Queen of Scots?

   b What religion did most people follow in Scotland?

   c Why was Mary chased out of Scotland by the Scottish nobles?

2 Read Source 2. Make a list of all the things that Parliament said Mary, Queen of Scots had done.

3 Parliament wanted to get rid of Mary. Elizabeth hesitated. Why did Elizabeth not want to execute Mary?

SOURCE 2

She has challenged the crown of England. She has made the Duke of Norfolk disobedient to your Majesty. She has stirred the Duke of Northumberland and Westmorland to rebel We, your true and obedient servants, do most humbly ask your Majesty to punish and correct all these treasons.

Parliament accusing Mary Queen of Scots in 1572.

A painting of Mary, Queen of Scots in 1578. She was 36 years old.

WAS MARY, QUEEN OF SCOTS INVOLVED IN A PLOT TO KILL ELIZABETH?

Many people suspected that Mary had plotted against Elizabeth for years. In 1586, Walsingham (one of Elizabeth's ministers) had proof that she was plotting against Elizabeth with a man called Babington.

This is what happened:

- Mary was imprisoned in Fotheringay Castle. She received letters from a Catholic called Anthony Babington. The letters were hidden in beer barrels.

- Babington wanted to kill Elizabeth. He would bring in Catholic armies from Europe to help. Then Mary could become queen.

- Mary replied to Babington saying that she would follow his plans.

- Walsingham discovered the letters.

- It has been suggested that Walsingham's spies forged the letters.

- Mary was put on trial for her part in the Babington plot. However, the court could not prove that the handwriting was Mary's.

- The court found her guilty of treason.

Activity Time

1 Imagine you have carried out an investigation into Mary, Queen of Scots. Was she part of the Babington plot to kill Elizabeth or not? Draw the chart below in your book.

Mary is guilty	Mary is innocent

Write down the things you think show Mary was guilty in one column. Write down the things you think show Mary was innocent in the other column. You will need to look at pages 140, 141 and 142.

2 You now need to advise Elizabeth on what to do with Mary, Queen of Scots. You have three options:

a set Mary free as long as she goes abroad

b keep her locked up for ever

c have her executed for treason.

Discuss your findings in class.

Question Time

1 Look at the Factfile on page 140. Write down one thing that shows you whether Mary, Queen of Scots was a wise ruler or not.

2 Look at the portrait in Source 3. How does the artist make Mary look:

a religious

b strong

c a victim?

3 Why would the Pope's excommunication of Elizabeth in 1570 make the Catholic threat even worse?

WHY DID PHILIP OF SPAIN POSE SUCH A BIG PROBLEM FOR ELIZABETH I?

The Catholic king, Philip II of Spain was one of the most powerful men in Europe. When Elizabeth came to the throne of England Philip offered to marry her. Instead of marriage, England and Spain drifted closer to war.

TIMELINE – THE STEPS TO WAR

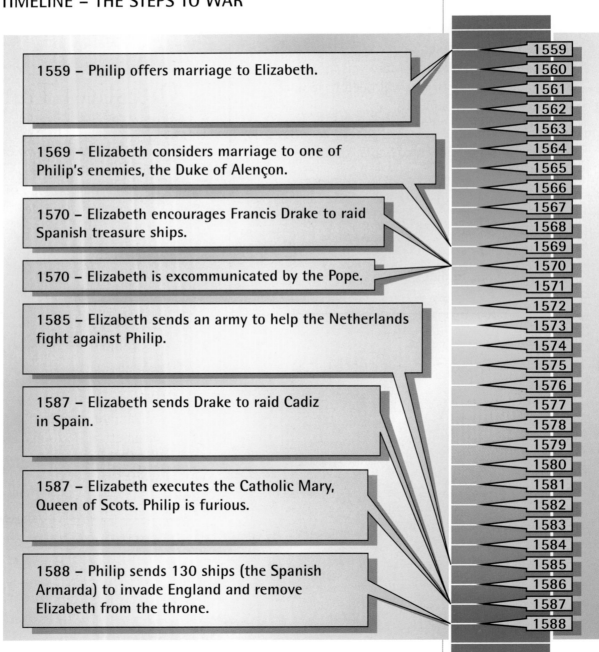

1559 – Philip offers marriage to Elizabeth.

1569 – Elizabeth considers marriage to one of Philip's enemies, the Duke of Alençon.

1570 – Elizabeth encourages Francis Drake to raid Spanish treasure ships.

1570 – Elizabeth is excommunicated by the Pope.

1585 – Elizabeth sends an army to help the Netherlands fight against Philip.

1587 – Elizabeth sends Drake to raid Cadiz in Spain.

1587 – Elizabeth executes the Catholic Mary, Queen of Scots. Philip is furious.

1588 – Philip sends 130 ships (the Spanish Armarda) to invade England and remove Elizabeth from the throne.

1559
1560
1561
1562
1563
1564
1565
1566
1567
1568
1569
1570
1571
1572
1573
1574
1575
1576
1577
1578
1579
1580
1581
1582
1583
1584
1585
1586
1587
1588

Activity Time

1 a Look at the graph below. Copy this into your book but make it larger. Label each of the main events from the timeline on page 144 along the bottom of the graph.

b Put a cross to show how the relationship between Elizabeth and Philip changed. Were they friends or enemies? One example has been done for you.

2 Look at your graph of Elizabeth and Philip's relationship. Label each event or cross to see whether it was to do with:

a personal life
b religion
c money
d power.

You could design a symbol for each type of event. For example a drawing of a heart could be the symbol for personal life.

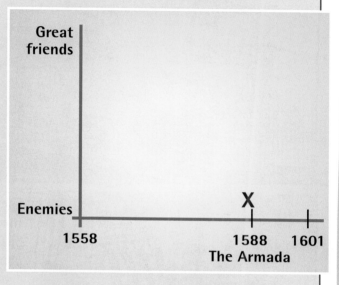

FIGHTING THE SPANISH

By 1588 Elizabeth's relations with Philip II had become very bad. Spain was one of the strongest countries in Europe. When a huge Spanish fleet (Armada) sailed to invade England, many people expected it to be successful. So why did it fail?

THE BACKGROUND

Elizabeth became queen in 1558. She refused to marry the Catholic Philip. In 1570 she was excommunicated by the Pope for being against Catholics. She executed the Catholic Mary, Queen of Scots in 1587. Elizabeth was a brave and determined woman, but was the defeat of the Spanish Armada really down to Elizabeth alone?

THE SPANISH FLEET LEAVES SPAIN FOR ENGLAND

There was a delayed start to the invasion because Francis Drake had destroyed many ships when he raided Cadiz.

The Duke of Medina, Sidonia, was put in charge of the Armada. He was seasick and hated the job. The Spanish delay meant that English were well prepared.

The Spanish were attacked by English fireships in the English Channel. To escape the fire, the Spanish ships cut their anchors. The Spanish ships were scattered and blown off course by a storm. The English then attacked them with cannons. Fifty English sailors were killed, but no ships were lost. The Spanish lost three ships and over 1000 men.

The Spanish could not land in the Netherlands. They had wanted a base there so they could pick up more soldiers and then invade England.

Elizabeth made a speech to her soldiers at Tilbury. She encouraged them to be brave.

The Spanish fleet faced storms as it tried to return home. Only about half the ships got back to Spain safely.

EFFECTS OF THE ARMADA

- The English celebrated the great victory.
- Elizabeth took much of the credit for the victory.
- The Spanish threat to Elizabeth's rule died down.
- Elizabeth carried on helping the Protestants in the Netherlands to fight against Philip.
- The Spanish worked hard to build up their navy. This stopped English sailors raiding Spanish ships so easily.

SOURCE 1

A portrait of Queen Elizabeth I, painted in 1588 to celebrate the defeat of the Spanish Armada.

Question Time

1. Why did the Spanish have a delayed start to the invasion of England?

2. How did the Spanish delay help the English?

3. How did the English attack the Spanish ships in the English Channel?

4. Why did the Spanish ships get scattered?

5. Look at page 147. How did Elizabeth make sure she was seen as the leader of England, even though she could not go to war because she was a woman?

6. Look at Source 1. What message does the portrait give us about Elizabeth and the Armada? How does the artist do this?

7. What did England gain from the defeat of the Armada?

HOW DID ELIZABETH DEAL WITH THE PROBLEM OF MARRIAGE?

MARRIAGE IN TUDOR TIMES

Wealthy young women did not usually choose who they would marry. The purpose of marriage was to produce heirs. Money and land were important parts of the marriage contract.

The average age of marriage for women was 20. Elizabeth came to the throne at the age of 24. She was expected to marry quite soon.

WHY WAS MARRIAGE A PROBLEM FOR ELIZABETH?

Elizabeth had to think about the future of the country as well as that of her family and herself.

Here are some of the things that she had to think about:

- What religion should her husband follow? Most of the foreign princes were Catholic. This would upset some Protestant groups in England, particularly the Puritans.

- Should she marry a foreigner?

- Should she marry an Englishman, as Parliament wanted her to do?

- Should she marry a member of a royal family or a nobleman?

SOURCE 1

A picture painted in 1601 showing Elizabeth and her courtiers.

WHAT PARLIAMENT WANTED

Parliament wanted Elizabeth to marry. This would bring an heir to the throne. Parliament was afraid that if Elizabeth died without an heir there would be civil war. The fighting would be about who would be the next monarch.

Many women in Tudor times died in childbirth. If Elizabeth died before she had made England a more safe and united country, there could be civil war.

Marriage to one person would make others jealous (either foreign princes or her own nobles). Elizabeth had learned from her cousin Mary Queen of Scots marriages that this could cause trouble.

Elizabeth made the most of her reputation as a virgin queen. She used it to make her special.

I am young enough to have many children but I have no plans yet.

Elizabeth let foreign princes and English nobles think that they might have a chance of marriage. It gave her power over them.

WHO WANTED TO BE KING OF ENGLAND?

Here are five of the main suitors.

Philip of Spain

- He was a Catholic, and was six years older than Elizabeth.

- He had been married to Elizabeth's half-sister, Mary I.

- He was one of the most powerful men in Europe. He ruled Spain, the Netherlands, Portugal and parts of South America.

Duke of Alençon

- He was the youngest brother of the King of France.

- He was short, pockmarked and 20 years younger than Elizabeth.

- He was Catholic but supported the Netherlands against Spain.

- Elizabeth enjoyed his company.

Robert Dudley, Earl of Leicester

- He was a childhood friend of Elizabeth.

- Elizabeth liked and trusted him.

- Elizabeth's liking for him meant jealousy from the other nobles.

- He would like to have married Elizabeth. His wife, Amy Robsart, died under mysterious circumstances.

Robert Devereux, Earl of Essex

- He was the stepson of the Earl of Leicester.

- He was 34 years younger than Elizabeth, and he was handsome and strong-willed.

- He was a brave soldier, and was popular with the people. He was very wealthy.

William, Prince of Orange

- Almost the same age as Elizabeth.

- Protestant leader of the rebellion in the Netherlands against Spain.

- He owned land in Germany, France and Holland.

Question Time

1 Why did Parliament want Elizabeth to marry?

2 What was Parliament afraid of if Elizabeth died without an heir to the throne?

3 Look at pages 150 and 151. Fill in the chart below to find out the strengths and weaknesses of each of Elizabeth's main suitors.

	Wealth and lands	Family and religion	Personality and looks	Popularity	Main strengths	Main problems
Philip II of Spain						
Duke of Alençon						
Earl of Leicester						
Earl of Essex						
Prince of Orange						

4 Look at what you have written in the chart. Who do you think Elizabeth should have married? Remember you have to think about the country, and not just Elizabeth.

5 Choose one of the other suitors. Write down one reason why it would have been unwise for Elizabeth to marry him.

WHAT HAPPENED TO THE FIVE SUITORS?

- Philip of Spain became an enemy of Elizabeth and tried to invade England.

- The Earl of Leicester fell out of favour with Elizabeth, but she gave him command of the English forces against the Spanish Armada. He was always unpopular in England and died in 1588.

- The Duke of Alençon died in 1584.

- The Earl of Essex disobeyed Elizabeth many times but she forgave him. He plotted against her chief ministers and was executed at the age of 34.

- William, Prince of Orange was assassinated in 1584.

LEAVING IT TOO LATE

By the time the Spanish Armada was defeated, Elizabeth was 54 years old. She was too old to have children. She had solved many of her problems and England was mostly a safe and united country. But what would happen to the throne of England after her death?

Question Time

1 Make a list of the benefits of Elizabeth not marrying.

2 Make a list of the problems of Elizabeth not marrying.

3 Do you think that Elizabeth should have married?

HOW DID ELIZABETH DEAL WITH THE PROBLEM OF POOR PEOPLE AND BEGGARS?

Today poor people get help from the government. There was no help for poor people in Elizabethan England. Should the government help poor people? Which poor people deserved to be helped?

THE PROBLEM OF POVERTY

More and more people were becoming poor in Elizabethan England. They no longer had monasteries to give them help. The changes in farming meant that the poor could no longer graze their animals on open common land. There was a lot more sheep-farming so fewer workers were needed. Prices were rising but wages were not, so the poor got poorer.

MORE AND MORE BEGGARS

About 10,000 out of 5 million people were making their living by begging or stealing.

- Some people were too old or too sick to work and had no one to look after them.

- Some people lost their jobs and could not find work.

- Some people were lazy and would not work.

Lazy, fit beggar

Injure yourself or your child

Pretend to be mad (Eat soap and so froth at the mouth)

Pretend to be injured

Steal washing from people's clothes lines to sell

SOURCE 1

A picture of different types of beggars in a sixteenth century book.

TWO DIFFERENT TYPES OF POOR

Elizabeth's government decided to sort poor people into categories:

- The deserving poor: sick people, old people and children.

- The undeserving poor: fit, able-bodied people who chose not to work.

ELIZABETH'S ACTION ON POVERTY

Henry VIII and Edward VI had already passed laws against beggars who were healthy and who could get work. They were often whipped or branded.

The problem of poverty was discussed in Parliament during Elizabeth's reign. Elizabeth and Parliament wanted to help genuine poor people and to punish dishonest poor people.

Money had to be found to help genuine poor people.

SOURCE 2

The poor are divided into three sorts:

- *The fatherless child, old, blind people, lame people and people with incurable diseases.*
- *People who have had an accident such as a wounded soldier.*
- *People who cannot save money, rioters, vagabonds and rogues who pretend to be ill.*

Taken from a book by William Harrison written in 1587.

SOURCE 4

The churchwardens and four well-off house owners shall be called overseers of the poor. They shall set to work children whose parents cannot keep them and also all married and unmarried persons who have no means to keep themselves.

Taken from the Tudor Poor Law.

SOURCE 3

- *Every parish will collect a poor rate (tax) to help the poor.*
- *Parishes can force able-bodied poor people to work.*
- *The poor must stay in their parish.*
- *Parishes are to look after the deserving poor.*

An extract from the 1601 Poor Law.

DID THE ELIZABETHAN POOR LAWS WORK?

Here are some opinions by historians:

- They did nothing to stop the poor being poor.

- They saved some people from starvation.

- The rich had to pay a lot of money to the poor.

- The population increased and there were bad harvests so lots of people stayed poor.

- They separated the deserving poor from the undeserving poor.

Question Time

1 The person in charge of giving out poor relief (money to the poor) in each parish was called the overseer. Would he have helped each of the characters below? Remember that they would have to be deserving poor to get money.

a A woman with a large family, seen begging in the local town with her children.

b A man whose leg had been mangled in an accident with a cart and who could not get a job.

c A man who had lost his job on a farm and wandered around looking for work, sometimes disguised as a cripple.

2 Read the section headed Did the Elizabethan Poor Laws work?

a Which of the opinions are positive about the Elizabethan Poor Laws?

b Which of the opinions are negative about the Elizabethan Poor Laws?

c Which is the odd one out?

3 Do we have the same problems in dealing with the poor today?

DID ELIZABETH SUCCESSFULLY SOLVE THE PROBLEMS THAT BESET HER DURING HER REIGN?

Some historians say that Elizabeth just avoided problems. She did not solve them.

Copy and fill in the chart below. You will need to collect evidence from your work in this Unit. Some of the columns are filled in for you.

Problem	Successful action	Problems that wouldn't go away	Marks out of 5 for overall success
Religious change	Set up Church of England	Extreme religious groups	
Catholics and Puritans			
Competition for the throne – Mary, Queen of Scots			
The Spanish threat			
A husband	Unmarried so no jealousy or foreign control	No direct heir	
Poor people in England		Did not end poverty	

Activity Time

❶ In pairs, design a poster to show:

- Elizabeth's problems

- Elizabeth's answers to the problems

- how successful she was in dealing with each problem.

Try to show which you think were the biggest problems for Elizabeth and which were the smaller ones.

Use all the information in this Unit for ideas.

❷ Compare your poster with the rest of the class. Are there any that have different ideas from yours? If so, why do you think that is?

❸ When Elizabeth died in 1603, her cousin King James VI of Scotland became King James I of England as well. Look at the chart you have filled in at the top of this page. What problems do you think James would have faced when he became king?

Unit 6: What were the achievements of the Islamic states 600–1600?

WHAT IS ISLAM?

In the Middle Ages, Islamic rulers created an empire which lasted for many centuries. People in this empire were held together by similar beliefs, laws and customs. Many of them spoke Arabic. Before we can investigate the achievements of this empire we need to understand more about Islam. The people who follow the religion of Islam are called Muslims. Nearly one-fifth of the people in the world today are Muslims.

THE BASIC BELIEFS OF ISLAM

The basic beliefs of Islam are the five Pillars of Islam. These are shown below.

The five Pillars of Islam.

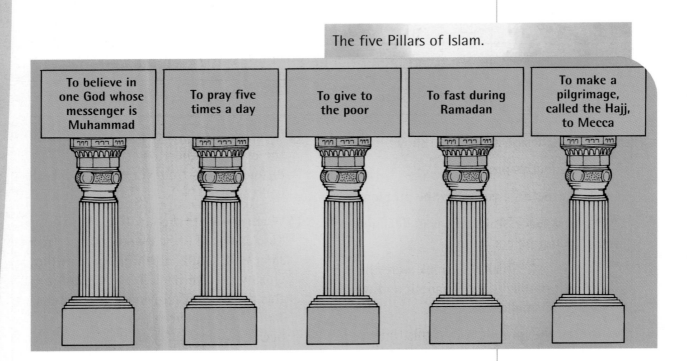

| To believe in one God whose messenger is Muhammad | To pray five times a day | To give to the poor | To fast during Ramadan | To make a pilgrimage, called the Hajj, to Mecca |

WHAT WAS PEOPLE'S RELIGION BEFORE ISLAM?

In the Middle East some people were Christian or Jewish. Many others worshipped many different gods.

WHO FOUNDED ISLAM?

Muhammad was born in Mecca in Arabia in 570AD. He started the religion of Islam. He became a prophet (a teacher who gives messages received from God).

WHAT HAPPENED AND WHEN?

When Muhammad was 40, Muslims believe that he began to receive messages from God in the form of poems. People began to listen to Muhammad's teaching. He became a highly respected leader. He advised people on every aspect of their lives.

WHAT HAPPENED TO ISLAM AFTER MUHAMMAD DIED?

The Qur'an

Muhammad's teachings were written down in Arabic after he died. They formed the Islamic Holy Book. It was called the Qur'an.

Hadith

Muslims also learn from Muhammad in a book called the Hadith. This includes examples from his life and many of his wise sayings.

Caliphs

Leaders, called caliphs, took over after Muhammad.

Activity Time

❶ Make a glossary page to collect key words that you come across in this Unit. You could set it out like the chart below. Start by filling in your glossary for the words given below.

Islamic history – Key Word	What does it mean?
Qur'an	
Hadith	

❷ Draw the five pillars of Islam shown on page 158. Muslims get their ideas from the Qur'an and the Hadith. They also follow the five Pillars of Islam, which are their basic beliefs. Muslims believe that all aspects of their life should be influenced by Muhammad's teachings.

❸ We are going to use many different historical sources in our investigation of the Islamic states. These include pictures, photographs and writings. Write down two problems that we might have with historical evidence about the Islamic states between 600 and 1600.

HOW DID THE WORLD OF THE MIDDLE EAST CHANGE DURING THE LIFE OF THE PROPHET MUHAMMAD AND THE FIRST FOUR CALIPHS?

WHAT HAPPENED DURING MUHAMMAD'S LIFETIME?

The messages Muhammad said he received from God included ideas that criticised the way the old leaders ruled. He was chased out of his home town of Mecca. He moved to Medina in 622.

Muhammad became leader in Medina. He ruled wisely. Many people became Muslim. This meant that Islam became strong enough to fight against the people from Mecca. In 630 the Muslims gained control of Mecca. Soon more conquests followed and the Muslim Empire grew.

WHAT HAPPENED AFTER THE DEATH OF MUHAMMAD?

The first four caliphs who ruled Muslim lands after Muhammad were his friends and relatives. They helped to spread Islam to new lands.

- First Caliph – Abu Bakr (632-4)

- Second Caliph – Umar (634-44) murdered

- Third Caliph – Uthman (644-56) murdered

- Fourth Caliph – Ali (656-61) murdered.

After the murder of Ali, there was a split between different groups of Muslims. One leader no longer ruled over all the Muslim Empire.

Question Time

1. Why did Muhammad leave Mecca?

2. How did Muhammad's leadership benefit Islam?

3. Add the word 'caliph' to your glossary and explain what it means.

WHERE WAS THE ISLAMIC EMPIRE?

The spread of the Islamic Empire during the sixth and seventh centuries.

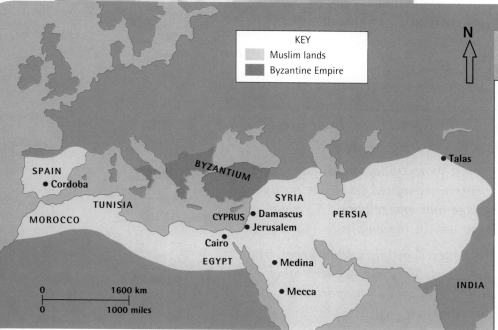

KEY
Muslim lands
Byzantine Empire

N

SPAIN
• Cordoba
TUNISIA
MOROCCO
BYZANTIUM
CYPRUS • Damascus
• Jerusalem
Cairo
EGYPT
SYRIA
PERSIA
• Medina
• Mecca
• Talas
INDIA

0 ——— 1600 km
0 ——— 1000 miles

Timeline of Islamic expansion

Islamic state in Medina.	625
Mecca gained by Medina Muslims.	630
Muslim armies gain Jerusalem, Damascus, Syria. and Persia.	640
Cairo invaded. Egypt gained.	642
Cyprus captured.	649
Tunisia and Morocco gained.	670
Muslim armies reach the borders of India.	707
Cordoba and part of Spain gained.	711
Central Asia becomes Muslim after the Battle of Talas.	751

Question Time

Make a large copy of this map.

a Colour in the Muslim Empire. Use a different colour for Byzantium. Put the colours in the key.

Look at the timeline on the right.

b Find each place on the map. Write the date it became Muslim under each place.

c How many kilometres does the empire stretch from east to west, and from north to south?

WHY WAS ISLAM SO SUCCESSFUL IN ITS EARLY YEARS?

Muslims believe that the main reason for the success of Islam is that it was what God wanted. Historians look at other reasons which may have helped the spread of Islam.

Factfile: The Success of Islam

Muslims should spread Islam. They should expand the empire. They should carry out jihad (holy war) against enemies. Soldiers who died fighting for Islam would go to heaven. Belief in heaven gave poor people hope for better things.

The old empires of Persia and Byzantium were weak. Muslim armies were well organised and disciplined. The soldiers were determined to win battles for God. The old empires and other tribes made themselves weak by fighting each other.

A large empire meant more trade, wealth and taxes. The tribes in the empire benefited from having one set of laws, one language and one religion. A strong empire meant peace within the empire.

Muslims treated conquered people with respect. They did not destroy buildings. They did not ban other religions. This gained Islam more support and converts (people who became Muslims).

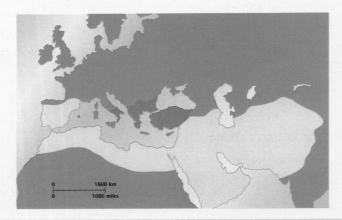

THE RULE OF THE CALIPHS

The first four caliphs of Islam became known as 'Rightly Guided Caliphs' because they followed closely the teachings of Muhammad.

Unlike Muhammad, they were not prophets. They did not claim to receive guidance from God. They followed Muhammad's teaching and they ruled wisely. They expanded the Islamic empire and gained people's respect.

SOURCE 1

In the name of God ... become Muslims and be saved. If not, accept our protection and pay taxes to us. Or else I shall come against you with men who love death as you love to drink wine.

A Muslim general wrote this to the leaders of Persian tribes in 636.

Factfile: Caliph Umar

A friend of Muhammad.

Ruled from 634 to 644.

Tall and gentle but some say had a temper.

Followed Muhammad's teachings.

Given the title 'Commander of the Faithful'.

Had few possessions and wore simple clothes

Encouraged Muslims to fight to protect Islam.

Let conquered Christians and Jews keep their religion.

Successfully invaded Jerusalem in 638.

Question Time

1 Look at the Factfile on page 162. Add the words 'jihad' and 'convert' to your glossary.

2 a Below is a list of some of the strengths of Islam and some of the weaknesses of its enemies. Sort them out and put them on the correct side of the cracker below:
- tribes fighting each other
- money from trade
- doing what God wanted
- older and weaker empires
- treating captured people well
- tribes with lots of different languages.

b Two boxes on each side should still be empty. Look at the Factfile on page 162. See if you can find two more causes for each side.

Strengths of Islam

Why was the spread of Islam so successful?

Weaknesses of enemies

3 How does Source 1 explain Muslim success in taking over new lands?

SOURCE 2

This peace guarantees them (Christians) safety, for their property, their churches and their crucifixes (crosses). They shall not be forced to change their faith.

From a treaty signed by Umar.

Question Time

1 List five qualities that you think make a good leader. Which is the most important?

2 Look at the Factfile on page 163.

a List all the qualities of Caliph Umar that would make him a good leader.

b Are there any qualities that might make him a poor leader?

c How many of his qualities are the same as the ones you have listed in Question 1?

d Compare your lists with other people's lists in your class.

3 Look at Source 2. Add crucifix to your glossary.

WELCOME TO BAGHDAD – CENTRE OF THE ISLAMIC EMPIRE

CITIES TELL YOU ABOUT PEOPLE

If you were able to build a brand new city, what would you want to include in it? Here are some things you might want – houses, sewers, churches, shops, entertainment centres, parks and sports facilities. Make a list of the things that you would include. Share your ideas with the rest of the class.

The things you and your class have chosen say something about what is important to people in the twenty-first century. We can look at the ancient city of Baghdad to find out what Islamic people wanted in those days.

FACTS ABOUT BAGHDAD

- It was founded in 762 and was the centre of the Muslim Empire until 1258.

- It was the second largest city in the world at that time (population 1.5 million).

- Over 100,000 men worked for four years to build it.

- It contained 1000 mosques, 65,000 public baths, sewers and clean water fountains.

- It had houses, palaces, markets, shops, gardens, hospitals, racetracks, a paper factory and an irrigation system to take water to the farms around the city.

- A House of Wisdom (University) was added in the ninth century.

SOURCE 1

The space between the middle and outer walls was left clear for defence. Between the middle and inner walls were the houses of the courtiers and army officers. Behind the inner walls lived the caliph's relatives and the most important officials. The hub of the city was the caliph's palace. Between the inner and middle walls each of the main streets became lined with all manner of shops making four central markets.

From a history book about Early Islam, written in the 1960s.

The round city of Baghdad.

Question Time

1 Copy out the drawing of the round city of Baghdad on page 165. Labels it with as much detail as you can.

2 We can find out how people lived in Early Islam by looking at ancient cities and reading history books. What sort of things can't we find out about?

EARLY BAGHDAD

Baghdad was founded by the Abbasid dynasty (family) in 762. This family were caliphs from 750 to 1055.

At the time of its greatest power, 1.5 million people lived in Baghdad. It was a centre of trade. Merchants visited Baghdad from all over the empire.

LATER BAGHDAD

Slowly the caliphs lost power as the army became more powerful.

Factfile: Baghdad

Trade

- *Traders or merchants came to Baghdad from as far away as China, Russia and Spain.*

- *There were many different souks (markets). They sold everything from pottery and leather goods to flowers and food.*

- *Market inspectors visited the stalls to check the quality and quantity of goods sold.*

- *The caliph employed a special trader to buy and sell for him. The caliph charged the traders tolls and rents in the markets (caliphs became very rich!).*

Arts, education and health

- *Houses and palaces were decorated with beautiful mosaics and tiles.*

- *The Qur'an encouraged education. There were libraries. One caliph built a House of Wisdom (a university).*

Food and entertainment

- *For the rich there was fish, chicken or lamb. Sauces were made from milk, herbs and nuts.*

- *Poor people ate rice bread and cheap meat.*

- *Women and children ate separately from the men.*

- *Going to the races was a popular form of entertainment.*

- *Men played chess, polo and archery.*

- *There were many parks and gardens in the city.*

Other work

- *Many people worked as merchants or traders but there were other jobs like shopkeepers, weavers, builders and keepers of mosques.*

- *The caliph employed many people as guards, police, soldiers, officials and servants.*

- *Rich people had slaves who were non-Muslim (often prisoners of war). They were treated well.*

- *If you were unwell you could visit one of the doctors who would treat you for a small fee.*

- *Regular washing was very important. People kept themselves clean for Allah (God). There were many public baths and fountains with clean water in the city.*

SOURCE 2

Near the mosque you will find the souk of the bookseller, the souk of the book binders, the souk of the leather merchants and the market of slippers.

Approaching the gates of the town you will find the makers of saddles ... Then the food sellers together with the basket makers.

At the edge of the town ... the dyers, the tanners, and almost outside the city limits, the potters.

Ibn Bututa, a visitor, describes the markets of Baghdad.

SOURCE 4

There are many public baths. Each has a number of private bathrooms. Each has a washbasin with taps supplying hot and cold water.

Every bather is given three towels. One is to wear around his waist when he comes out and the other two to dry himself.

Ibn Bututa describes Baghdad's public baths.

SOURCE 3

A twelfth century manuscript picture showing wealthy men being entertained in a garden in Baghdad.

Timeline

The army has more power than the caliphs.	*850*
Persia rules Baghdad but the army still has power.	*945*
Turkish Muslims, called the Seljuk Turks, invade Baghdad.	*1055*
Mongols sack (destroy) the city of Baghdad. The last caliph is murdered. The Islamic lands are no longer one united empire.	*1258*

SOURCE 5

A picture of the Mongol siege of Baghdad in 1258, drawn in Persia in the fifteenth century.

Question Time

1 Look at the Factfile on trade on page 166. What is a souk? Add souk to your glossary.

2 Look at the Factfile on arts, education and health on pages 166–7.

a What was a House of Wisdom?

b What does Allah mean? Add this word to your glossary.

3 Look at Source 2.

a Which souks or markets are found nearest the mosque?

b Which souks are found near the gates of the town?

c Which souks are found at the edge of the town?

4 Look at Source 5.

a Make a list of what you can see inside and outside the walls.

b Is there enough evidence in the picture to convince you that it is Baghdad? Explain your answer.

Activity Time

You have been asked to design a booklet showing people the splendour of Baghdad in the eleventh century. In your booklet you must include:

a a plan of the layout of the city

b a list of what you can buy in the markets

c a list of where the markets are

d a list of entertainment

e what to do if you are ill.

ISLAMIC THINKING – MATHS AND SCIENCE

Look at the words in the box below. You may need a dictionary to help you find the meaning of these words.

chemistry	average	zero	sodium	alkali	algebra

All these words come from Arabic. The Islamic religion encouraged learning. Famous books by Greek and Roman thinkers were translated into Arabic. These books were studied in the universities and libraries. As a result of this learning, many Muslims came up with new ideas and discoveries.

PROGRESS IN MATHEMATICS

The decimal system of counting is based on Arabic changes to an old Hindu method. Muslims also developed new theories in algebra and geometry. Muslims used their mathematical skills in practical ways such as in building, daily worship and trade.

SOURCE 1

- *Seek knowledge, even as far as China.*

- *The ink of the scholar is more sacred than the blood of the martyr (a person who dies for their religion).*

Two sayings of Muhammad about learning.

PROGRESS IN SCIENCE

Progress in science included the areas of medicine, alchemy (chemistry) and astronomy. Muslim thinkers studied the planets and stars. They developed a Greek tool used for measuring the distance to stars and planets. It was called the astrolabe. The astrolabe was used by travellers to tell their position by the stars. Muslim scientists also developed the magnifying lens.

Muslim thinkers translated Greek books on medicine by doctors like Galen. They developed the study of medicine much further.

Question Time

❶ Add meanings for the following words to your glossary: chemistry, average, zero, sodium, alkali, algebra, decimal, geometry, martyr.

❷ Look at the words in the box on page 170. What do these words have in common? Think about who uses these words.

Arabic numbers

Helped to make calculations easier.

Alchemy

Science of how chemicals work, for example which chemicals can be used to make dyes and glazes.

Astrolabe

Helped to tell the time. Helped travellers to work out where they were. Used to find the direction of Mecca and the times for daily prayers.

Question Time

1 Read Source 1 on page 170. How does this show us that Muhammad was wise?

2 Muslims developed many ideas and tools. Look at the three drawings on page 171 and read the boxes below them. Now produce a report which shows how important the Muslim ideas are to the study of science. Use this chapter and your school library for help.

Think about the following in your report.

a How do calculations help science?

b What is alchemy? Why is it important?

c Why was the astrolabe important? What do we use today? You can use pictures to illustrate your report.

WHAT CAN WE LEARN FROM THE ARCHITECTURE OF ISLAMIC CIVILISATIONS?

The word for the design of buildings is architecture. Islamic buildings are some of the most beautiful in the world. Examples include:

- the Taj Mahal in India (Source 5, page 15).
- Córdoba in Spain (Source 2)
- the Alhambra Palace in Spain (Sources 5 and 6, page 174).

THE FEATURES OF A MOSQUE

Most mosques have similar features. These features are related to the religious purpose of the building.

SOURCE 2

The inside of the mosque at Córdoba.

SOURCE 3

A photograph of the ouside of the mosque at Edirne.

SOURCE 4

Arabesque is the term used to describe the pattern of flowing lines with flowers and leaves.

ISLAMIC ART

Islamic art is based on geometric shapes and calligraphy (fine writing), rather than paintings of people and animals. This is because Islamic teachers said that because God is the only creator, man should not make images of living things.

MOST MOSQUES HAVE THESE FEATURES

Minaret	tower from where the people are called to prayer
Dome	to represent the power of heaven over Earth
Courtyard	central garden with buildings around it
Fountain	for people to wash themselves before praying
Decoration	decorated arches with carving and geometric shapes.

Question Time

1 Look at the box above which explains the features of mosques. Look at Sources 2 and 3. Which features can you see?

2 Add the following words to your glossary:

calligraphy, arabesque, minaret.

3 Why did mosques have domes?

THE MUSLIMS IN SPAIN

The Muslims invaded Spain in 711 and remained there for several hundred years. They were finally chased out of Spain by the Christians at the end of the fifteenth century.

MUSLIM BUILDINGS IN SPAIN

Source 2 shows the mosque at Córdoba. Córdoba was the capital of Muslim Spain. Sources 5 and 6 show parts of the Alhambra Palace in Granada in Spain. It took over 100 years to build.

SOURCE 5

The Alhambra Palace in Spain. The photograph shows strong walls and towers.

SOURCE 6

Part of the Alhambra Palace in Spain. It has beautiful gardens and fountains.

Question Time

What can Islamic buildings tell us about the Muslims who planned and built them?

a Look at the diagram on page 165, Source 5 on page 169 and Source 5 on this page. Write two or three sentences saying what these buildings tell us about the fears of the Muslims who planned them.

b Look at Source 2 on page 172, and Source 3 on page 173. Write two or three sentences saying what these buildings tell us about the religious feelings of the Muslims who planned them.

c Look at the diagram on page 165, Source 3 on page 168, Source 5 on page 169 and Source 6 on this page. Write two or three sentences saying what these buildings tell us about the way in which Muslims liked to live.

HOW SUCCESSFUL WERE CRUSADER ATTACKS AGAINST THE ISLAMIC WORLD?

The headline suggests Jerusalem was in the headlines recently, much as it was in the Middle Ages. It is a city that was, and still is, fought over. But why?

Peace talks in Middle East hit crisis – what is the future of Jerusalem? 9/4/99

JERUSALEM THE HOLY CITY

Jerusalem is a holy city for Jews, Christians and Muslims. This is because Jerusalem contains the following sacred monuments.

- The Wailing or Western Wall. This is the remaining wall of part of the Holy Temple. This is a site of pilgrimage and prayer for Jews.

- The Church of the Holy Sepulchre. This is thought be built on the site of Jesus' tomb. This is a site of pilgrimage and prayer for Christians.

- The Dome of the Rock Mosque. This is where Muhammad is said to have ascended to heaven. This is a site of pilgrimage and prayer for Muslims.

Many pilgrims visited Jerusalem in the past and they still do today. When Caliph Umar (a Muslim) took over Jerusalem in 638, he allowed the Christians and Jews freedom to worship. A few hundred years later, however, Muslim Turks stopped this freedom of worship.

THE CRUSADES

The Crusades were holy wars. The Crusaders were Christians. They wanted to capture the Holy Land (the land around Jerusalem) from the Muslims. We need to answer quite a few questions before we can understand the importance of Jerusalem and the Crusades:

- What were the Crusades?

- Who were the Crusaders?

- Where did the Crusaders come from?

- Why did the Crusaders attack?

- What did the Crusaders want?

- What did the Crusaders do?

- What happened to the Muslims?

- What was, and still is, so important about who rules Jerusalem?

THE FIRST CRUSADE – 1095

During the eleventh century, Muslims from Turkey began to move west. By 1076 they had captured Jerusalem. These Muslim Turks did not agree with Christian pilgrims visiting Jerusalem. They treated them badly, often robbing and sometimes murdering them. This made Christians everywhere very angry.

Pope Urban II made a famous speech in 1095. He asked for Christian soldiers to join together to win back the holy city of Jerusalem. Thousands of people travelled from all over Europe to fight against the Saracens (the Crusader name for the Muslims). Some of the Christian soldiers won land and settled in the Holy Land. Some returned home. Some were killed. Christian kingdoms were set up around Antioch, Edessa, Jerusalem and Tripoli. Some of these kingdoms lasted for 200 years.

Activity Time

How successful were the Crusader attacks against the Islamic world?

The word 'How' in the question means that we need to try to work out whether the attacks were very/quite/not very/not at all successful. Make a list of three different things that we could look at in order to decide how successful the Crusaders' attacks were. One example could be the amount of land captured by the Christians.

Overview of the Crusades

- The Crusades spanned almost 200 years.

- At first the Christians gained a lot of land.

- The Christians and Muslims did not always fight. There were long periods of peace.

- Christians and Muslims swapped ideas. Christians brought the discoveries of the Muslims back to Europe.

FOUR EVENTS THAT SHOW HOW FAR THE MUSLIMS WERE THREATENED BY THE CHRISTIANS

1099 – The capture of Jerusalem

The Crusaders reached Jerusalem in June 1099. They were short of water and supplies. It took them a month to break through the walls of Jerusalem. Once in control of the city, many Crusaders looted gold and silver and murdered thousands of Jewish and Muslim men, women and children.

SOURCE 2

A fourteenth century picture showing Crusaders attacking the walls of Jerusalem.

SOURCE 1

A siege machine throwing heads into a town.

Question Time

1. Look at Source 2. What weapons are being used to break through the walls of Jerusalem?

2. Look at Source 1. Why do you think the Crusaders are hurling chopped off heads over the walls?

3. What would people think of the Crusaders after they attacked Jerusalem? (Think about Christians, Jews and Muslims.)

1187 – The Battle of Hattin

By this time the Muslims had begun to win back land. They were led by Salah al-Deen (Saladin), the famous Turkish sultan and leader of the Muslims.

Salah al-Deen took over the town of Tiberias and won the Battle of Hattin. After the battle he ordered all the Christian knights to be killed. He then took over the holy city of Jerusalem. When he captured Jerusalem he did not murder any of the Christians. He either took ransom money or sold them to become slaves.

1198 – The Fourth Crusade

Richard I of England had led a Third Crusade. He won back Acre and Jaffa, but he failed to take Jerusalem. This meant that a Fourth Crusade was needed.

During the Fourth Crusade the Crusaders captured Constantinople. Constantinople was held by Greek Christians who had taken it from the rightful emperor. Instead of handing Constantinople back to the emperor, the Crusaders kept the city for themselves. This showed the Crusaders as a selfish army.

Question Time

1. What is the name of the Muslim leader who won at the Battle of Hattin?

2. Why do you think Salah al-Deen executed all the Christian knights after the Battle of Hattin?

3. Why do you think Salah al-Deen did not execute the Christians in Jerusalem?

4. Write out the sentence below and complete it.
   The actions of the Fourth Crusaders looked bad because they

   _____

   _____

An artist's reconstruction of the siege of Constantinople.

SOURCE 3

The Crusader States were on their last legs. They were difficult to reinforce because Jerusalem was no longer in Christian hands. There were no able-bodied pilgrims to stay and fight. At the same time the standard of living rose and people were better off staying where they were.

Some reasons for the end of Christian rule in the Holy Land, from a recent school book.

Question Time

1 What two reasons does Source 3 give for the end of Christian rule in the Holy Land?

2 'The fall of Acre' is the name the Christians gave to the battle when they lost. What name would the Muslims have given to the same battle?

1291 – The fall of Acre

Acre was the very last town held by the Christians. They had ruled there for 100 years. The Muslims outnumbered the Christians by five to one. It did not take them long to capture Acre.

This was the end of Christian rule in the Holy Land. But the Crusaders did carry on going on Crusades in places such as Spain and Prussia.

Activity Time

1 Look back at pages 177 to 179 and fill in the four main events on a copy of the flagpole below. For each event show whether it was a victory for the Muslims or Christians. Some events could have benefits for both Muslims and Christians.

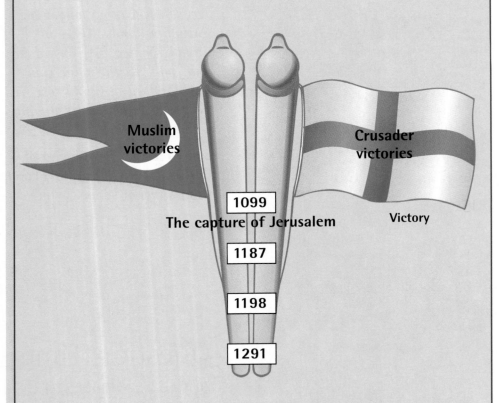

Muslim victories

Crusader victories

1099
The capture of Jerusalem

Victory

1187

1198

1291

2 Read the sentences below and answer True or False.

- The capture of Constantinople in 1198 was a victory for the Crusaders but it was not a Christian victory.

- Constantinople was taken by the Muslims in 1198.

- The capture of Constantinople helped the Muslims because they stayed in Constantinople and did not attack Jerusalem.

3 How successful would you say that the Crusader attacks were? Use the flagpole timeline to help you.

WHY DO PEOPLE DISAGREE ABOUT SALAH AL-DEEN?

Was Salah al-Deen a great military leader or was he a tyrant?
Historians disagree, so see what you think.

SALAH AL-DEEN AND THE BATTLE OF HATTIN

Salah al-Deen's most famous battle was the Battle of Hattin (see page 178). He was a clever fighter. He attacked the Crusaders when they were marching in the hot desert. They were very short of water and very tired. They were easily defeated. Winning the Battle of Hattin meant that Salah al-Deen took back Jerusalem.

WINNING JERUSALEM

After the Battle of Hattin, Salah al-Deen executed the Crusader army. Some people say this was cruel. Some people say that it was a wise move to make. When Salah al-Deen captured Jerusalem, he allowed the Christians there to live. Some people criticised him for this. Other people said it was an example of how fair and tolerant he was.

KEEPING JERUSALEM

When the Crusaders came back on the Third Crusade, Salah al-Deen defended Jerusalem so well that Richard I of England and his army could not capture it.

FAMOUS IN EAST AND WEST

King Richard I asked people to pay tax to pay for the Third Crusade. English people called this the Saladin Tithe.

Salah al-Deen died of yellow fever in 1193. 100 years later the Muslims finally defeated the Crusaders. Salah al-Deen had been very important in regaining much land for the Muslims.

Who was Salah al-Deen?

Salah al-Deen was the Sultan (leader) of Egypt. He fought:

- *to regain the Holy Land*
- *to push the Christians from the Middle East*
- *to defeat rival Muslim groups*
- *to capture all of Egypt and Syria.*

Question Time

1. Add the word 'sultan' and its meaning to your glossary.
2. Why was Salah al-Deen a clever fighter?
3. What did Salah al-Deen gain by winning the Battle of Hattin?
4. Why do you think Salah al-Deen is so important in the history of the Crusades?

WHAT DID PEOPLE AT THE TIME THINK OF SALAH AL-DEEN?

SOURCE 1

Some of the prisoners were kept safe until Salah al-Deen had decided what to do with them. The rest were sent to heaven in a quick and merciful death by the sword. Among the prisoners was Reynald of Chatillon. The tyrant (Salah al-Deen) cut off his proud head with his own hands. This was either because he was in a rage, or possibly out of respect for so great a man. He ordered the fighting monks to be beheaded. He was determined to wipe them out for he knew they were stronger than him in battle.

An English monk writing about the Battle of Hattin in 1200.

SOURCE 2

God made straight for the sultan the road leading to his enemies' destruction. If his only achievement was this one victory then he would still be above all the kings of former times, let alone those of his age.

Salah al-Deen's secretary writing about Salah al-Deen's victory at the Battle of Hattin.

SOURCE 3

A painting showing Salah al-Deen taking the Holy Cross.

SOURCE 4

I never saw him find the enemy too powerful. He would think carefully ... and take the necessary steps, without becoming angry. At the Battle of Acre, the centre of the Muslim army was broken, but he stood firm with a handful of men and led them into battle again.

Salah al-Deen's military skill, as described by his offical Baha al-Din

Question Time

1 Look at Source 1.

a How were Crusader prisoners killed?

b Why did Salah al-Deen cut off Reynald of Chatillon's head himself?

c What are the good things that the monk says about Salah al-Deen?

d What are the bad things that the monk says about Salah al-Deen?

2 Read Sources 2 and 4.

a Who wrote Source 2?

b Are you surprised at what he says about Salah al-Deen? Why?

c Who wrote Source 4?

d Are you surprised at what he says about Salah al-Deen? Why?

3 Fill in the chart below to sum up what people at the time thought of Salah al-Deen

Source	Written by Muslim or Christian?	Salah al-Deen shown as positive (as a good leader) or negative (as a bad leader)?

WHAT DO PEOPLE LATER IN HISTORY THINK OF SALAH AL-DEEN?

SOURCE 5

Salah al-Deen was a great warrior, but he was not rough and unmannerly. Even among people with high standards of good manners, Salah al-Deen stood out for his courtesy. To the Arabs, the Crusaders must have seemed rough and barbarous.

From *Pilgrimages and Crusades* by G Evans (1976).

SOURCE 6

In the nineteenth century the German Kaiser (Emperor) built a marble tomb for Salah al-Deen at the place where he is buried. This was to celebrate his life.

This was 700 years after Salah al-Deen's death.

SOURCE 7

A painting of Salah al-Deen with Saddam Hussein, the President of Iraq.

Question Time

Look at Sources 5-7.

1 Fill in the chart below.

Source	Who wrote it or made it?

2 Each of the sources shows something different about Salah al-Deen. Copy and complete each of the sentences below.

- In Source 5, Salah al-Deen is shown as a ————————————— man.
- In Source 6, Salah al-Deen is shown as a ————————————— man.
- In Source 7, Salah al-Deen is shown as a ————————————— .

3 Salah al-Deen's reputation seems to have changed over the centuries. Here are some reasons why this might have happened. Which do you think are the most likely reasons?

a New evidence has been found which proves that Salah al-Deen was a good man and never cruel.

b Christians at the time realised that he had beaten them and so could not see his good qualities.

c His battles are exciting stories which make him famous in any time period.

d Today people can see that the Muslim culture was more advanced than the Christian one at the time of Salah al-Deen. This makes people think that Salah al-Deen was a skilled and well-mannered man.

RULING THE OTTOMAN EMPIRE

The Ottomans were Muslims from Turkey who took over many of the Islamic states in about 1400. They created the Ottoman Empire, which lasted until 1924 (see map on pages 186–7).

HOW DID THE OTTOMANS BECOME (AND STAY) SO SUCCESSFUL?

The Ottomans were very successful because:

Ingredient No. 1 – One famous capital city.

The Ottoman ruler, Sultan Mehmet II captured Constantinople in 1453. It was a vital trading place and a gateway to the Ottoman Empire. Mehmet renamed the city Istanbul.

Ingredient No. 2 – A fine fighting force.

The Ottomans captured Christian boys and trained them to be highly skilled soldiers (they had to become Muslims). This saved having to pay men to join the army.

The Ottomans developed a fine navy and advanced weapons.

The Ottomans paid pirates from North Africa to fight for them.

Ingredient No. 3 – Magnificent wealth and beautiful buildings.

Sultan Mehmet II built fine buildings in Constantinople. He employed many people in his palace. His kitchens were so big that over 1000 people worked there.

Ingredient No. 4 – Strict laws all over the empire.

The Ottomans had strict laws. The Sultan had judges who used the Qur'an to make their decisions.

Punishments were severe. You could have your hand chopped off for stealing.

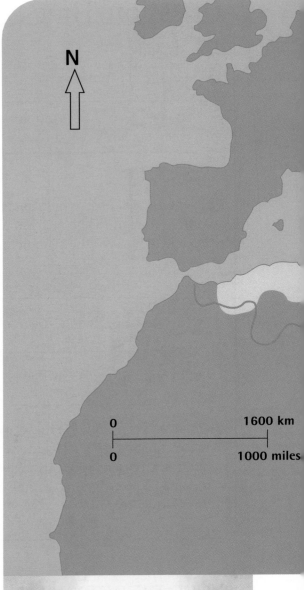

This map shows the growth of the Ottoman Empire.

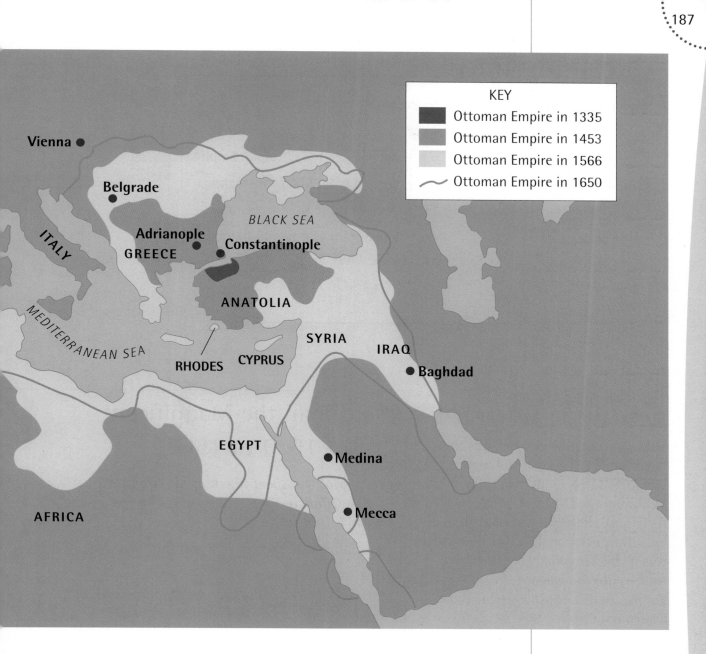

Vienna ●

Belgrade ●

Adrianople ●
GREECE

BLACK SEA

Constantinople ●

ITALY

ANATOLIA

RHODES
CYPRUS
SYRIA
IRAQ
Baghdad ●

MEDITERRANEAN SEA

EGYPT

Medina ●

Mecca ●

AFRICA

KEY
■ Ottoman Empire in 1335
■ Ottoman Empire in 1453
■ Ottoman Empire in 1566
〜 Ottoman Empire in 1650

SOURCE 1

Mehmet chose the best place in the middle of the city and ordered a mosque to be built there to rival the biggest and finest in height, beauty and size.

Written by Kritovoulus, Mehmet II's biographer, after the capture of Constantinople.

Question Time

Look at the sentences below. Match the heads to the tails.

- Constantinople was a
- The Ottoman laws were
- The Ottoman judges
- The Ottomans
- One punishment was

- The Ottomans had a

- fine navy with advanced weapons.
- gateway to the Ottoman Empire.
- cutting off a hand for stealing.
- were fair and used the Qur'an.
- had an army of highly trained Christians.
- very strict.

THE GOLDEN AGE OF SULEYMAN THE MAGNIFICENT

Suleyman the Magnificent was the most famous Ottoman sultan. He conquered new lands, and under Suleyman the Ottoman Empire was at its largest and richest. It gained great wealth from trade. This was because it was at the crossroads of the busiest trade routes between Asia and Europe. Here are just a few of the traded goods:

- silk from Persia (Iraq)
- porcelain from China
- woollen cloth from England
- spices from India.

Suleyman the Magnificent (ruled 1520 to 1566)

- *Warrior: he spent much of his life at war. The Ottoman Empire was at its largest by the end of his reign.*

- *Law maker: he was very fair and made many laws.*

- *Employer: he employed clever, hard-working men to make sure the empire was well run.*

- *Patron: he spent a great deal of money on building palaces, on paintings and on other luxuries such as beautiful carpets and china.*

- *Family man: one of his wives was called Roxelana. She wanted her son to be Suleyman's heir. She persuaded Suleyman that his oldest son (the true heir) was not to be trusted. Suleyman had his oldest son killed. Roxelana's son, Selim II became sultan after Suleyman's death. He was not a good leader and spent his time eating, drinking and having a good time. After him the sultans were less powerful.*

SOURCE 2

Suleyman was famous all over the world as a great leader. He lived from 1499 to 1566. This was at a similar time to Henry VIII of England (1491–1547).

SOURCE 3

A painting of King
Henry VIII in the
sixteenth century.

Henry VIII – a similar ruler to Suleyman?

- *Henry VIII ruled for 38 years.*

- *He worked to make England powerful.*

- *He was helped by clever advisers.*

- *He broke away from the Pope and set up his own Church of England.*

- *This gave English monarchs power over religion as well as politics and money.*

- *He spent money on feasts, paintings, clothes and entertainment.*

- *He had six wives in his effort to have a son to succeed him.*

- *His son Edward VI was weak and died young.*

- *He was popular with most people of England.*

- *He was ruthless and killed anyone who went against him.*

- *He made England important.*

- *He did not gain much extra land.*

- *He has gone down in history as a tyrant.*

SOURCE 4

This photograph is of the inside of Suleyman's mosque at Edirne, built in the sixteenth century.

Question Time

1 The mosque shown on page 172 was built at Córdoba in Spain. It was built many years before the mosque shown in Source 4 (opposite). Make a list of the similarities between the two mosques.

2 Compare Henry VIII with Suleyman the Magnificent. You will need to look at pages 188, 189 and 190. Make a list of the similarities between the two men, for example:

Henry VIII and Suleyman the Magnificent both:

- ruled for a long time
- had more than one wife.

3 Now make a list of the differences between Henry VIII and Suleyman the Magnificent.

1000 YEARS OF ISLAMIC CIVILISATION, 600–1600

You are part of a team working on an internet encyclopaedia for 11 to 13 year-olds. You are going to write a web page to describe the main aspects of Islamic civilisation. Your web pages should look good, but also contain lots of helpful information.

INSTRUCTIONS

Your web page should include four different parts:

1   Include an introduction saying why this period of Islamic history is so important in world history.

2   Write several paragraphs about different aspects of Islamic civilisation. Here are some suggestions to choose from:

architecture	mathematics and science	making an empire
famous cities	way of life of the Ottomans	the Crusades
famous Muslims	caliphs	religion

3   Choose, from this Unit, one picture to go with the writing. Explain what it shows about Islamic achievements.

4   Choose another picture for the title page. It should sum up the achievements made by the Islamic states in this period. Under the picture you will need to finish this sentence: 'For me this picture sums up what the Islamic Empire achieved between 600 and 1600 because ...'

Pick out the main points that you want to include. You could copy and paste your pictures from an encyclopaedia. You could create arrows and label different parts of your picture.